PRACTICAL CONVERSATION GUIDE

English - Spanish

EDITORIAL
arguval

Cover and illustrations: Luis Ojeda

© Purificación Blanco Hernández
© **Editorial ARGUVAL**
C/ María Malibrán, 16
29590 MÁLAGA
ISBN: 978-84-86167-99-8
Depósito legal: MA-461-2015
E-mail: editorial@arguval.com
http://www.arguval.com

Impreso en España - Printed in Spain
Imprime Imagraf

INDEX

HOW TO USE THIS GUIDE

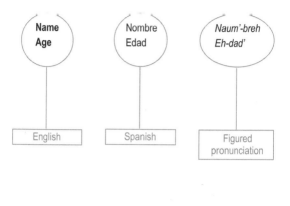

Name Age	Nombre Edad	*Naum'-breh* *Eh-dad'*
English	Spanish	Figured pronunciation

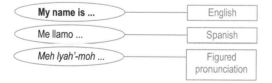

My name is ...	English
Me llamo ...	Spanish
Meh lyah'-moh ...	Figured pronunciation

FIGURED PRONUNCIATION

Spanish words are pronounced exactly as they are written, except for a few exceptions (the silent *h* and the two symbols *b/v* for the same sound).

So, we can say that the pronunciation is not at all difficult; nevertheless, we offer you a figured pronunciation based on comparisons with English sounds for a practical use, if lacking the scientific exactness of the International Phonetic Alphabet.

Vowels

	Like in...	Represented by...
a	*father*	*ah*
e	*bed, they*	*eh*
i	*tip, fee*	*e, ee*
o	*August*	*au, oh*
u	*food*	*oo*

Consonants with special difficulty

	Like in...	
b, v	*bomb*	*b*
c	*thin* (before e, i)	*th*
	cat (before a, o, u)	*c*
g	*host* (before e, i)	*h*
	go (before a, o, u)	*gh*
h	always silent	
j	*host* (stronger *h*)	*h*
ll	*million*	*ly*
ñ	*onion*	*ny*
q	*king*	*k*
r	*road* (final or interior)	*r*
	strongly trilled	*r-r*
	(when doubled or initial)	
y	*yes, day* (when final)	*y*
z	*thin*	*th*

In **diphthongs** you pronounce every single vowel:

	Like in...	Represented by...
au	cow	*ow*
ei	say	*ey*
ia	yacht	*ya*
ie	yes	*ye*
iu	few	*ew*
oi	boy	*oy*
ui	winter	*wi*
ue	well	*we*
ua	wallet	*wa*

STRESS

Words ending in a *vowel*, in *n* or in *s*, are stressed on the next of the last syllable: *mesa, orden, niños.*

Words ending in *any other consonant* are stressed on the last syllable: *señor, Madrid, general.*

If a word does not conform with these two rules, an acute accent (´) is written over the vowel of the stressed syllable: *café, capitán, inglés, Málaga.*

In this Guide it is represented by (´).

A SHORT GUIDE TO SPANISH GRAMMAR

1. ARTICLES

The definite article

Before a masculine noun, *sing.* **el** *libro* (the book).

pl. **los** *libros* (the books).

Before a feminine noun*, *sing.* **la** *casa* (the house).

pl. **las** *casas* (the houses).

When the article *el* comes after the prepositions *de* (or or from) or *a* (to), a contraction takes place: *de el = del, a el = al.*

Before adjectives with abstract meaning the neuter form **lo** is used: **lo** *bello* (the beautiful, what is beautiful).

The indefinite article

Before a masculine noun, *sing.* **un** *hombre* (a man).

pl. **unos** *hombres* (some men).

Before a feminine noun*, *sing.* **una** *mesa* (a table).

pl. **unas** *mesas* (some tables).

*The forms *el, un* are used before a feminine noun beginning with the stressed sound *a* or *ha*: *el agua fresca* (the fresh water), *un hacha afilada* (a sharp axe).

2. NOUNS

Gender

Nouns belong either to the masculine or the feminine gender. The natural gender is maintained in nouns like: *el padre* (father), *la madre* (mother); *el rey* (king), *la reina* (queen); *el toro* (bull), *la vaca* (cow).

Nouns ending in *-o* are generally masculine: *el vino* (wine). Exceptions: *la mano* (hand), *la foto* (photo), *la moto* (motorbike).

Nouns ending in *-a, -ción, -sión, -dad, -tad* are feminine: *la ventana* (window), *la habitación* (room), *la ciudad* (town).

Exceptions: *el día* (day), *el tranvía* (tram) and nouns of Greek origin ending in *-ma*: *el clima* (climate), *el problema* (problem).

There are no special rules for nouns ending otherwise: *el mes* (month), *la flor* (flower), *el autobús* (bus), *la miel* (honey).

Number

The plural of nouns is formed by adding *-s* to nouns ending in un-stressed vowel or stressed *-é*: *puerta* (door), *puertas* (doors); *café* (coffee shop), *cafés* (coffee shops).

Nouns terminating in consonant add *-es*: *tren* (train), *trenes* (trains); *color* (colour), *colores* (colours). The letter *z* is replaced by *c* before *-es*: *luz* (light), *luces* (lights).

Masculine plural forms may refer to a mixed set of both masculine and feminine: *los padres* (parents), *los hermanos* (brothers and sisters), *los chicos* (boys and girls).

3. ADJECTIVES

Adjectives agree with their nouns in gender and number. Adjectives and nouns are inflected alike; e. g. *He comido una naranja muy buena* (I have eaten a very good orange); *estos plátanos son muy buenos* (these bananas are very good).

If adjectives end in -o, they have 4 forms: *malo, mala, malos, malas* (bad).

Adjectives not ending in -o have only 2 forms: *verde, verdes* (green); *fácil, fáciles* (easy).

Exception: The adjectives denoting a nationality, with 4 forms: *inglés, inglesa, ingleses, inglesas*.

Adjectives generally follow their noun: *corbata azul* (blue tie).
Some adjectives standing before a masculine singular noun lose their final vowel or syllable:
bueno: *un buen vino* (a good wine).
malo: *mal tiempo* (bad weather).
primero: *el primer piso* (the first floor).
tercero: *el tercer hombre* (the third man).
grande: *un gran palacio* (a big palace).
Santo: *San Pedro* (Saint Peter).

Comparison of adjectives

The comparative of superiority is formed with *más ... que* (more ... or -er than); that of inferiority, with *menos ... que* (less ... than); that of equality, with *tan ... como* (as/so ... as).

The relative superlative is rendered by prefixing the definite article to the comparative of superiority: *el más largo* (the longest), *la más guapa* (the more beautiful).

The absolute superlative is formed by prefixing the adverb *muy* to the adjective or by adding to it the ending *-ísimo*: *muy bueno* or *buenísimo* (very good).

*Some adjectives have special forms: *mejor* (better), *peor* (worse), *mayor* (greater, larger, older), *menor* (smaller, younger).

4. PRONOUNS

A pronoun replaces a noun in a sentence. Certain pronouns as e. g. the posessive, demonstrative, interrogative and indefinite pronouns have the same form and meaning as the corresponding adjectives, which are followed by a noun.

PERSONAL PRONOUNS

yo (I)	*me* (me)	*mí** (me)
tú (you)	*te* (you)	*ti** (you)
él (he)	*le* (him), *lo* (him, it)	
ella (she)	*le* (her), *la* (her, it)	
usted* (you)	*le*	
nosotros/as (we)	*nos* (us)	
vosotros/as (you)	*os* (you)	
ellos/as (they)	*les, los, las* (them)	
ustedes* (you)	*les*	

*Usted (*Vd.*) and *ustedes* (*Vds.*) are used when you want to be more formal (similar to using Mr. … or Ms. … instead of first names) and take the verb in the third person.

The personal subject pronouns do not normally appear with the verb, because its forms indicate the subject by themselves; nevertheless, *Vd.* and *Vds.* appear more frequently than other pronouns: *Usted no tiene razón* (You're not right).

The object pronouns precede the verb, except when it is an infinitive, a gerund or an affirmative imperative; e. g. *Te espero* (I'm waiting for you), but *Démelo* (Give it to me).

*Mí and *ti* are used when a preposition precedes.

REFLEXIVE PRONOUNS differ from the objective forms only in the third person (sing. and plur.): *Se lava* (he/ she washes himself/herself), but *Me lavo* (I wash myself).

POSSESSIVE ADJECTIVES AND PRONOUNS

mi, mis (my)	*mío, -a, -os, -as* (mine)
tu, tus (your)	*tuyo, -a, -os, -as* (yours)
su, sus (his, her, its)	*suyo, -a, -os, -as* (his, hers, its)
nuestro, -a, -os, -as (both: our and ours)	
vuestro, -a, -os, -as (both: your and yours)	
su, sus (their)	*suyo, -a, -os, -as* (their)

In case of ambiguity instead of *su, suyo* a paraphrase is used: *su carta*: la carta de él (de ella, de usted, de ellos, de ellas, de ustedes).

DEMONSTRATIVE ADJECTIVES AND PRONOUNS

Spanish divides space into 3 separate planes: *aquí* (the area which is relatively close to the speaker), *ahí* (an intermediate area which is near the hearer) and *allí* (the area distant for both, the speaker and the hearer). Consequently, there are 3 kinds of demonstrative adjectives and pronouns:

este, esta, esto*, estos, estas (this, these)
ese, esa, eso*, esos, esas (that, those -near you-)
aquel, aquella, aquello*, aquellos, aquellos (that, those there)

**Esto, eso, aquello* are neuter pronouns and are used to refer to something when we do not know what it is or we do not wish to mention its name.

RELATIVE AND INTERROGATIVE ADJECTIVES AND PRONOUNS

quien, quienes (who)   *¿quién/quiénes?* (who?)

que (who, which, that)   *¿qué?* (what?)

el/la cual, los/las cuales (which) *¿cuál/cuáles?* (which one-s?)

All interrogative adjectives and pronouns bear a written accent mark to distinguish them from the corresponding relative.

An inverted question mark is put at the beginning of the interrogative sentence in written Spanish.

INDEFINITE ADJECTIVES AND PRONOUNS

cada, cada uno (each/every, everyone)

otro, -a, -os, -as (other, another)

todo, -a, -os, -as (all, whole)

todo el mundo (everybody)

varios, -as (several)

mucho, -a, -os, -as (much, many)

demasiado, -a, -os, -as (too, too much, too many)

*alguno, -a, -os, -as** (some, any)

*ninguno, -a** (no, none)

alguien (somebody, anybody)

algo (something, anything)

nadie (nobody)

nada (nothing)

poco, -a, -os, -as (little, few)

*cualquiera** (any, whoever, whichever)

*When preceding a masculine noun, the short forms *algún, ningún* are used. Also *cualquier* before a noun (masc. or femin.).

5. ADVERBS

Many adverbs are formed from adjectives by adding the suffix *-mente* to the feminine form: *solamente* (only), *normalmente* (normally).

In compound tenses, the adverb cannot take its place between the auxiliary and the participle, as in English: *Ya ha venido/Ha venido ya* (He has already come).

According to the meaning, they are the following kinds of adverbs in Spanish:

of time

hoy (today)	*ayer* (yesterday)
mañana (tomorrow)	*otra vez* (again)
antes (before)	*después* (after, afterwards)
ya (already)	*todavía* (still, yet)
temprano (early)	*tarde* (late)
ahora (now)	*luego* (later)
pronto (soon)	*entonces* (then)
pasado mañana (the day after tomorrow)	*anteayer* (the day before yesterday)

of frequency

siempre (always)	*nunca* (never)
algunas veces (sometimes)	*a menudo* (often)
una vez (once)	*dos veces* (twice)
alguna vez (ever)	*normalmente* (usually)
muchas veces (many times)	

of degree

casi (nearly, almost)	*muy* (very)
bastante (quite, fairly)	*apenas* (hardly)
totalmente (totally)	

of manner

bien (well)	*despacio* (slowly)
mal (badly)	*rápidamente* (quickly)

and most of the adverbs ending in *-mente*.

of place

aquí (here)	*delante* (in front of)
ahí (there)	*detrás* (behind)
allí (over there)	*enfrente* (opposite)
cerca (near)	*arriba* (up, upstairs)
lejos (far, away)	*abajo* (down, downstairs)
alrededor (around)	*dentro* (in, inside)
en todas partes (everywhere)	*fuera* (out, outside)

of probability

quizá (maybe, perhaps)
posiblemente (possibly)
probablemente (probably)
a lo mejor (probably)

of affirmation/negation

sí (yes)
no (no)
en absoluto (not at all)
por supuesto (of course)
verdaderamente (indeed)

relative

cuando (when)
donde (where)
por que, por lo que (why)

interrogative

¿cuándo? (when?)
¿dónde? (where?)
¿por qué? (why?)

6. PREPOSITIONS

a (to, at)

acerca de (about, concerning)

además de (besides, in addition)

al lado de (beside, next)

con (with)

contra (against)

de (of, from)

desde (from, since)

durante (during)

en (in, on, into)

entre (between, among)

hacia (towards)

hasta (till, until)

junto a (close, next to)

para (for, in order to)

por (because of, along)

respecto a (in relation to)

según (according to)

sin (without)

sobre (on, over, about)

7. CONJUNCTIONS

y (and)

o (or)

ni (nor, neither)

también (also, too, as well)

tampoco (not ... either)

pero (but)

sin embargo (nevertheless)

para que (so that)

como (as, since)

cuando (when)

mientras (while, whereas)

porque (because)

si (if, whether)

ni siquiera (not even)

aunque (although)

entonces (then)

8. VERBS

According to the termination of the infinitive, Spanish verbs fall into three conjugations: 1. verbs ended in -ar, as *hablar* (to speak); 2. verbs ending in -er, as *comer* (to eat); 3. verbs terminating in -ir, as *vivir* (to live).

All verbal terminations are added to the radical which you get by omitting the ending -ar, -er, -ir respectively.

COMPOUND TENSES are formed by means of the corresponding tense of the auxiliary verb *haber* (to have) (see List of Irregular Verbs) and the past participle of the verb that is conjugated: *He trabajado* (I have worked).

The NEGATIVE CONJUGATION is rendered by placing the adverb *no* before the verb: *No hablo* (I do not speak).

The INTERROGATIVE CONJUGATION is obtained by placing the subject after the verb: *¿Está Elena?* Is Helen in?

REGULAR VERBS

Infinitive	Gerund	Past Participle
habl/ar	habl/ando	habl/ado
com/er	com/iendo	com/ido
viv/ir	viv/iendo	viv/ido

INDICATIVE

Present

habl/o, -as, -a, -amos, -áis, -an
com/o, -es, -e, -emos, -éis, -en
viv/o, -es, -e, -imos, -ís, -en

Simple Past

habl/é, -aste, -ó, -amos, -asteis, -aron
com/í, -iste, -ió, -imos, -isteis, -ieron
viv/í, -iste, -ió, -imos, -isteis, -ieron

Imperfect Past

habl/aba, -abas, -aba, -ábamos, -abais, -aban
com/ía, -ías, -ía, -íamos, -íais, -ían
viv/ía, -ías, -ía, -íamos, -íais, -ían

Future

hablar/é,	
comer/é,	-ás, -á, -emos, -éis, -án
vivir/é,	

Conditional

hablar/ía,	
comer/ía,	-ías, -ía, -íamos, -íais, -ían
vivir/ía,	

IMPERATIVE

habl/a, -e, -emos, -ad, -en
com/e, -a, -amos, -ed, -an
viv/e, -a, -amos, -id, -an

SUBJUNCTIVE

Present

habl/e, -es, -e, -emos, -éis, -en
com/a, -as, -a, -amos, -áis, -an
viv/a, -as, -a, -amos, -áis, -an

Past

habl/ara, -aras, -ara, -áramos, -arais, -aran   or
habl/ase, -ases, -ase, -ásemos, -aseis, -asen

com/iera,	
com/iese,	-ieras, -iera, -iéramos, -ierais, -ieran or
viv/iera,	-ieses, -iese, -iésemos, -ieseis, -iesen
viv/iese,	

IRREGULAR VERBS

In this short summary of the most usual verbs, irregular forms are indicated in italics and it does not appear regular tenses.

SER (to be; also auxiliary for the passive voice)
Pres. *soy, eres, es, somos, sois, son*
Past Simp. *fui, fuiste, fue, fuimos, fuisteis, fueron*
Imperfect. *era, eras, era, éramos, erais, eran*

HABER (to have; used only as an auxiliary verb)
Pres. *he, has, ha, hemos,* habéis, *han*
Future. *habré, habrás, habrá, habremos, habréis, habrán*

ESTAR (to be, to be in, to stand, to be present)
Pres. *estoy, estás, está,* estamos, estáis, *están*
Past Simp. *estuve, estuviste, estuvo, estuvimos, estuvisteis, estuvieron*

TENER (to have, to have got, to possess)
Pres. *tengo, tienes, tiene,* tenemos, tenéis, *tienen*
Past Simp. *tuve, tuviste, tuvo, tuvimos, tuvisteis, tuvieron*
Future. *tendré, tendrás, tendrá, tendremos, tendréis, tendrán*

HACER (to do, to make)
Pres. *hago,* haces, hace, hacemos, hacéis, hacen
Past Simp. *hice, hiciste, hizo, hicimos, hicisteis, hicieron*
Future. *haré, harás, hará, haremos, haréis, harán*

DECIR (to say, to tell)
Pres. *digo, dices, dice,* decimos, decís, *dicen*
Past Simp. *dije, dijiste, dijo, dijimos, dijisteis, dijeron*
Future. *diré, dirás, dirá, diremos, diréis, dirán*

IR (to go)
Pres. *voy, vas, va, vamos, vais, van*
Past Simp. *fui, fuiste, fue, fuimos, fuisteis, fueron*
Imperfect. *iba, ibas, iba, íbamos, ibais, iban*

VENIR (to come)

Pres. *vengo, vienes, viene*, venimos, venís, *vienen*

Past Simp. *vine, viniste, vino, vinimos, vinisteis, vinieron*

Future. *vendré, vendrás, vendrá, vendremos, vendréis, vendrán*

SALIR (to go out, to leave, to depart)

Pres. *salgo*, sales, sale, salimos, salís, salen

Future. *saldré, saldrás, saldrá, saldremos, saldréis, saldrán*

SABER (to know)

Pres. *sé*, sabes, sabe, sabemos, sabéis, saben

Past Simp. *supe, supiste, supo, supimos, supisteis, supieron*

Future. *sabré, sabrás, sabrá, sabremos, sabréis, sabrán*

QUERER (to want, to wish, to love, to like)

Pres. *quiero, quieres, quiere*, queremos, queréis, *quieren*

Past Simp. *quise, quisiste, quiso, quisimos, quisisteis, quisieron*

Future. *querré, querrás, querrá, querremos, querréis, querrán*

9. NUMBERS

1. Uno. *Oo'-noh*
2. Dos. *Daus*
3. Tres. *Trehs*
4. Cuatro. *Kwa'-troh*
5. Cinco. *Theen'-coh*
6. Seis. *Seys*
7. Siete. *Sye'-teh*
8. Ocho. *Au'-choh*
9. Nueve. *Nweh'-beh*
10. Diez. *Dyeth'*

11. Once. *Aun'-theh*
12. Doce. *Dau'-theh*
13. Trece. *Treh'-theh*
14. Catorce. *Cah-taur'-theh*
15. Quince. *Keen'-theh*
16. Dieciséis. *Dye-the-seys'*
17. Diecisiete. *Dye-the-sye'-teh*
18. Dieciocho. *Dye-the-au'-choh*
19. Diecinueve. *Dye-the-nweh'-beh*
20. Veinte. *Beyn'-teh*

21. Veintiuno. *Beyn-te-oo'-noh*
22. Veintidós. *Beyn-te-daus'*
23. Veintitrés. *Beyn-te-trehs'*
24. Veinticuatro. *Beyn-te-kwa'-troh*

30. Treinta. *Treyn'-tah*
40. Cuarenta. *Kwa-rehn'-tah*
50. Cincuenta. *Thin-kwen'-tah*
60. Sesenta. *Seh-sehn'-tah*
70. Setenta. *Seh-tehn'-tah*
80. Ochenta. *Au-chehn'-tah*
90. Noventa. *Nau-behn'-tah*

100. Cien. *Thyen'*
200. Doscientos. *Daus-thyen'-tohs*
300. Trescientos. *Trehs-thyen'-tohs*
400. Cuatrocientos. *Kwa-troh-thyen'-tohs*
500. Quinientos. *Kee-nyen'-tohs*
600. Seiscientos. *Seys-thyen'-tohs*
700. Setecientos. *Seh-teh-thyen'-tohs*
000. Ochocientos. *Au-choh-thyen'-tohs*
900. Novecientos. *Noh-be-thyen'-tohs*

1.000. Mil. *Meel*
2.000. Dos mil. *Daus' meel*
5.000. Cinco mil. *Theen'-coh meel*
10.000. Diez mil. *Dyeth' meel*
100.000. Cien mil. *Thyen' meel*
1.000.000. Un millón. *Oon mil-lyaun'*
2.000.000. Dos millones. *Daus' mil-lyoh'-nehs*

1st. Primero. *Pre-meh'-roh*
2nd. Segundo. *Seh-goon'-doh*
3rd. Tercero. *Ter-theh'-roh*
4th. Cuarto. *Kwar'-toh*
5th. Quinto. *Keen'-toh*
6th. Sexto. *Sex'-toh*
7th. Séptimo. *Sep'-te-moh*
8th. Octavo. *Auk-tah'-boh*
9th. Noveno. *Nau-beh'-noh*
10th. Décimo. *Deh'-the-moh*

1/2. Medio. *Meh'-dyo*
1/3. Un tercio. *Oon ter'-thyo*
1/4. Un cuarto. *Oon kwar'-toh*
1/5. Un quinto. *Oon keen'-toh*
1/10. Un décimo. *Oon deh'-the-moh*

WEIGHTS AND MEASURES

Length
1 centímetro (cm) = 0,3937 inch = 0,0328 foot
1 metro (m) = 3,2808 feet = 1,0936 yards
1 kilómetro (km) = 0,6213 mile

Weight
1 kilogramo (kg) = 2,2050 pounds

Capacity
1 litro (l) = 0,212 gallon = 1,756 pints

Temperature
0° C = 32° F

To convert Fahrenheit into Celsius first deduct 32 and then multiply by 5/9.

EVERYDAY LIFE

Good morning
Buenos días
Bweh'-nohs dee'-ahs

Good afternoon
Buenas tardes
Bweh'-nahs tar'-dehs

Good evening
Buenas tardes/noches
*Bweh'-nahs tar'-dehs/
nau'-chehs*

Good night
Buenas noches
Bweh'-nahs nau'-chehs

Hello
Hola
Au'-lah

Goodbye
Adiós
Ah-dyos'

See you later/soon
Hasta luego/pronto
As'-tah lweh'-goh/praun'-toh

See you tomorrow
Hasta mañana
As'-tah mah-nyah'-nah

How are you?
¿Cómo está usted?
Cau'-moh es-tah' oos-ted'?

How are you?
¿Cómo estás?/¿Qué tal?
Cau'-moh es-tahs'?/Keh' tahl?

How's it going?
¿Cómo te va?
Cau'-moh teh bah?

I'm fine, thanks
Estoy bien, gracias
Es-toy byen, grah'-thyas

(Very) well/All right
(Muy) bien
(Moo'-y) byen

Not too bad, thanks
No me va mal, gracias
Noh meh bah mal, grah'-thyas

How about you?
Y tú ¿qué tal?
Ee too', keh' tahl?

How is your family?
¿Cómo está su/tu familia?
Cau'-moh es-tah' soo/too
fah-mee'-lya?

I am glad
Me alegro
Meh ah-leh'-groh

Nice to see you again
Me alegro de volver a verle/verte
Meh ah-leh'-groh deh baul-ber' ah ber'-leh/ber'-teh

It has been a long time!
¡Cuánto tiempo sin verle/verte!
Kwan'-toh tyem'-poh sin ber'-leh/ber'-teh!

How do you feel today?
¿Cómo se encuentra/te encuentras hoy?
Cau'-moh seh en-kwehn'-trah/teh en-kwehn'-trahs oy?

Give my regards to everybody
Recuerdos a todos
Reh-kwer'-dohs ah tau'-dohs

Give my love to the children
Besos a los niños
Beh'-sohs ah lohs nee'-nyohs

INTRODUCTIONS

Mr. (...)	Señor (Sr.) ...	*Seh-nyaur '...*
Mrs. (...)	Señora (Sra.) ...	*Seh-nyau'-rah ...*
Mr. and Mrs. (...)	Los señores (...)	*Lohs seh-nyau'-res...*
Sir	Señor	*Seh-nyaur'*
Madam	Señora	*Seh-nyau'-rah*

What is your name?
¿Cómo se llama Vd./te llamas?
Cau'-moh seh lya'-mah oos-ted'/
teh lyah'-mas?/

My name is ...
Me llamo ...
Meh lyah'-moh ...

Pleased to meet you
Encantado/a
En-can-tah'-doh/-ah

How do you do?
Mucho gusto
Moo'-choh goos'-toh

This is Mr ...
Este es el señor ...
Es'-teh es el seh-nyaur' ...

This is Mrs ...
Esta es la señora ...
Es'-tah es lah seh-nyau'-rah ...

Let me introduce you ...
Le/te presento a ...
Leh/teh preh-sen'-toh ah ...

I'd like to introduce you to ...
Quiero presentarle/te a ...
Kye'-roh preh-sen-tar'-leh/teh ah ...

Have you already met Mr ...?
¿Conoce ya al señor ...?
Cau-nau'-theh yah ahl seh-nyaur' ...?

Are you Mr/Mrs ...?
¿Es usted el señor/la señora ...?
Es oos-ted' el seh-nyaur'/lah seh-nyau'-rah ...?

Yes, I am he (she)
Sí, soy yo
See', soy yoh

Name	Nombre	*Naum'-breh*
Surname	Apellido	*Ah-peh-lyee'-doh*
Age	Edad	*Eh-dad'*
Marital status	Estado civil	*Es-tah'-doh the-beel'*
Single	Soltero/a	*Saul-teh'-roh/-ah*
Married	Casado/a	*Cah-sah'-doh/-ah*
Divorced	Divorciado/a	*De-baur-thya'-doh/-ah*
Widow(er)	Viudo/a	*Bew'-doh/-ah*
Profession	Profesión	*Prau-feh-syon'*
Address	Dirección/Domicilio	*De-rec-thyon'/Doh-me-thee'-lyo*

Identity card	**Passport**
DNI	Pasaporte
Deh-ehneh-ee'	*Pah-sah-paur'-teh*

Date of birth	**Place of birth**
Fecha de nacimiento	Lugar de nacimiento
Feh'-chah deh nah-the-myen'-toh	*Loo-gar deh nah-the-myen'-toh*

What is your name?
¿Cómo se llama usted?/¿Cuál es su nombre?
Cau'-moh seh lyah'-mah oos-ted'?/Kwal' es soo naum'-breh?

Where are you from?/What is your nacionality?
¿De dónde es usted?/¿Cuál es su nacionalidad?
Deh daun'-deh es oos-ted'?/Kwal' es soo nah-thyo-nah-le-dad'?

What is your name?
¿Cómo te llamas?/¿Cuál es tu nombre?
Cau'-moh teh lyah'-mahs?/Kwal' es too naum'-breh?

Where are you from?/What is your nacionality?
¿De dónde eres?/¿Cuál es tu nacionalidad?
Deh daun'-deh eh'-rehs?/Kwal' es too nah-thyo-nah-le-dad'?

What is your address?/Where do you live?
¿Cuál es su/tu dirección?/¿Dónde vive(s)?
Kwal' es soo/too de-rec-thyon'?/Daun'-deh bee'-beh(s)?

I'm from ...
Soy de ...
Soy deh ...

I was born in ...
Nací en ...
Nah-thee' en ...

What is your phone number?
¿Cuál es su/tu número de teléfono?
Kwal' es soo/too noo'-meh-roh deh teh-leh'-fau-noh?

What's your e-mail address?
¿Cuál es su/tu correo electrónico?
Kwal' es soo/too caur-reh'-oh eh-lec-trau'-nee-coh?

How old are you?
¿Cuántos años tiene(s)?
Kwan'-tohs ah'-nyohs tye'-neh(s)?

FAMILY

Boyfriend/girlfriend	Novio/a	*Noh'-byo/-ah*
Brother/sister	Hermano/a	*Er-mah'-noh/-ah*
Brother/sister-in-law	Cuñado/a	*Coo-nyah'-doh/-ah*
Cousin	Primo/a	*Prec'-moh/-ah*
Daughter-in-law	Nuera	*Nweh'-rah*
Father	Padre	*Pah'-dreh*
Father/mother-in-law	Suegro/a	*Sweh'-groh/-ah*
Grandfather	Abuelo	*Ah-bweh'-loh*
Grandmother	Abuela	*Ah-bweh'-lah*
Grandparents	Abuelos	*Ah-bweh'-lohs*
Grandson	Nieto	*Nye'-toh*
Granddaughter	Nieta	*Nye'-tah*
Husband	Esposo (marido)	*Es-pau'-soh (mah-ree'-doh)*

Mother	Madre	*Mah'-dreh*
Nephew/niece	Sobrino/a	*Sau-bree'-noh/-ah*
Parents	Padres	*Pah'-drehs*
Son/daughter	Hijo/a	*Ee'-hoh/-ah*
Son-in-law	Yerno	*Yer'-noh*
Uncle/aunt	Tío/a	*Tee'-oh/-ah*
Wife	Esposa (mujer)	*Es-pau'-sah/ (moo-her')*
Relatives	Parientes	*Pah-ryen'-tehs*
Acquaintance	Conocido/a	*Cau-nau-thi'-doh/-ah*

Do you have any brothers or sisters?
¿Tienes hermanos?
Tye'-nehs er-mah'-nohs?

Yes, I've got an elder brother
Sí, tengo un hermano mayor
See', ten'-goh oon er-mah'-noh mah-yaur'

Do you have any children?
¿Tienes hijos?
Tye'-nehs ee'-hohs?

Yes, I've got two kids
Sí, tengo dos niños
See', ten'-goh daus nee'-nyohs

ARRANGING TO MEET

Are you up to anything this evening?
¿Qué haces esta tarde/noche?
Keh' ah'-thehs es'-tah tar'-deh/nau'-cheh?

Have you got any plans for this evening/the weekend?
¿Tienes algún plan para esta tarde/el fin de semana?
Tye'-nehs al-goon' plan pah'-rah es'-tah tar'-deh/el feen deh seh-mah'-nah?

Are you perhaps free tomorrow afternoon?
¿Estás libre mañana por la tarde?
Es-tahs' lee'-breh mah-nyah'-nah paur lah tar'-deh?

What would you like to do this evening?
¿Qué te gustaría hacer esta tarde/noche?
Keh teh goos-tah-ree'-ah ah-ther' es'-tah tar'-deh/nau'-cheh?

Do you want to go somewhere at the weekend?
¿Quieres ir a algún sitio el fin de semana?
Kye'-rehs eer ah al-goon' see'-tyo el feen deh seh-mah'-nah?

What about going for a walk?
¿Qué te parece si vamos a dar un paseo?
Keh teh pah-reh'-theh see bah'-mohs ah dar oon pah-seh'-oh?

Would you like to join me for something to drink?
¿Quieres acompañarme a tomar algo?
Kye'-rehs ah-caum-pah-nyar'-meh ah toh-mar' al'-goh?

Sure	**I'd love to**
Sí, claro	Me encantaría
See, clah'-roh	*Meh en-can-tah-ree'-ah*

I'm too tired
Estoy demasiado cansado/a
Es-toy deh-mah-sya'-doh can-sah'-doh/-ah

I'm staying in tonight
Me quedaré en casa esta noche
Meh keh-dah-reh' en cah'-sah es'-tah nau'-cheh

I'm very busy at the moment
Ahora estoy muy ocupado/a
A-au'-rah es-toy moo'-y au-coo-pah'-doh/-ah

What date would be suitable?
¿Qué día te vendría bien?
Keh dee'-ah teh ben-dree'-ah byen?

What time shall we meet?	**At nine o'clock**
¿A qué hora quedamos?	A las nueve en punto
Ah keh' au'-rah keh-dah'-mohs?	*Ah lahs nweh'-beh en poon'-toh*

Where would you like to meet?
¿Dónde quieres que nos encontremos?
Daun'-deh kye'-rehs keh naus en-caun-treh'-mohs?

I'll see you at ten o'clock in the … pub
Nos vemos a las diez en el bar …
Naus beh'-mohs ah lahs dyeth' en el bar …

See you there!
¡Nos vemos allí!
Naus beh'-mohs ah-lyee'!

Let me know if you cannot make it
Avísame si no puedes venir
Ah-beeh'-sah-meh see noh pweh'-dehs beh-neer'

I'll call you later
Te llamo luego
Teh lyah'-moh lweh'-goh

I'm running a little late
Llegaré un poco tarde
Lyeh-gah-reh' oon pau'-coh tar'-deh

I'll be there in ... minutes
Estaré allí en ... minutos
Es-tah-reh' ah-lyee' en … me-noo'-tohs

Have you been waiting long?
¿Llevas mucho tiempo esperando?
Lyeh'-bahs moo'-choh tyem'-poh es-peh-ran'-doh?

Sorry for the delay	**That's fine**
Perdón por la tardanza	No pasa nada
Per-daun' paur lah tar-dan'-thah	*Noh pah'sah nah'-dah*

Who is it?
¿Quién es?
Kyen' es?

What is that?
¿Qué es eso?
Keh' es eh'-soh?

Where is it?
¿Dónde está?
Daun'-deh es-tah'?

Why?
¿Por qué?
Paur keh'?

Which one?
¿Cuál?
Kwal'?

How much/many?
¿Cuánto/-a/-os/-as?
Kwan'-toh/-ah/-ohs/-ahs?

Are you sure?
¿Seguro?
Seh-goo'-roh?

Really?
¿De verdad?
Deh ber-dad'?

OK?
¿Vale?
Bah'-leh?

All right (OK)
De acuerdo (Vale)
Deh ah-kwer'-doh (bah'-leh)

Yes
Sí
See'

No
No
Noh

That's right
Es verdad
Es ber-dad'

Of course
Por supuesto
Paur soo-pwehs'-toh

You are right
Tiene usted razón
Tye'-neh oos-ted' ah-thaun'

I see
Ya entiendo
Yah en-tyen'-doh

Not at all
En absoluto
En ab-sau-loo'-toh

That depends
Depende
Deh-pen'-deh

Never
Nunca
Noon'-cah

Nothing
Nada
Nah'-dah

It is wrong
No es así
Noh es ah-see'

I do not think so
No creo
Noh creh'-oh

MORE COMMON EXPRESSIONS

Thank you very much
Muchas gracias
Moo'-chas grah'-thyas

You are welcome
De nada
Deh nah'-dah

Please
Por favor
Paur fah-baur'

It is a pleasure
Con mucho gusto
Caun moo'-choh goos'-toh

Pardon
Perdón
Per-daun'

Excuse me
Disculpe
Dis-cool'-peh

Sorry
Perdón/Lo siento
Per-daun'/Loh syen'-toh

Welcome!
¡Bienvenido/a!
Byen-beh-nee'-doh/-ah!

Cheers!
¡Salud!
Sah-lood'!

Bless you!
¡Jesús!/¡Salud!
Heh-soos'!/Sah-lood'!

Good luck
¡Suerte!
Swer'-teh!

Happy birthday!
¡Feliz cumpleaños!
Feh-leeth' coom-pleh-ah'-nyos!

Congratulations
¡Felicidades!/¡Enhorabuena!
Feh-le-the-dah'-des!/En-au'-rah-bweh-nah!

Merry Christmas!
¡Feliz Navidad!
Feh-leeth' nah-be-dad'!

Happy New Year!
¡Feliz Año Nuevo!
Feh-leeth' ah'-nyoh nweh'-boh!

Sleep well!
¡Que duerma(s) bien!
Keh dwer'-mah(s) byen!

Same to you
Igualmente
E-gwal'-men-teh

Great!
¡Genial!
Heh-nyal'!

Well done!
¡Bien hecho!
Byen' eh'-choh!

What a pity!
¡Qué pena!
Keh' peh'-nah!

Don't worry!
¡No se/te preocupe(s)!
Noh seh/teh preh-au-coo'-peh(s)!

One moment, please
Un momento, por favor
Oon mau-men'-toh, paur fah-baur'

Have you got a minute?
¿Tiene(s) un minuto?
Tye'-neh(s) oon me-noo'-toh?

Calm down
Cálmese/Cálmate
Cal'-meh-seh/Cal'-mah-teh

Take your time
Tómate tu tiempo
Tau-mah-teh too tyem'-poh

It's up to you
Como quiera(s)
Cau'-moh kye'-rah(s)

No problem
No pasa nada
Noh pah'sah nah'-dah

What's the matter?
¿Qué pasa?
Keh' pah'-sah?

That's fine
Está bien
Es-tah' byen

Is anything wrong?
¿Pasa algo malo?
Pah'sah al'-goh mah'-loh?

Is everything OK?
¿Está todo bien?
Es-tah' tau'-doh byen?

Are you sure?
¿Está(s) seguro/a?
Es-tah'(s) seh-goo'-roh/-ah?

Don't forget
No se/te olvide(s)
Noh seh/teh aul-be'-deh(s)

That's enough
Es suficiente
Es soo-fe-thyen'-teh

It does not matter
No importa
Noh im-paur'-tah

Thanks for your help
Gracias por su/tu ayuda
*Grah'-thyas paur soo/too
ah-yoo'-dah*

Help yourself
Sírvase usted mismo/a
*Seer'-bah-seh oos-ted'
mees'-moh/-ah*

Here you are
Aquí tiene
Ah-kee' tye'-neh

You are very kind
Es usted muy amable
Es oos-ted' moo'-y ah-mah'-bleh

May I help you?
¿Puedo ayudarle?
Pweh'-doh ah-yoo-dar'-leh?

I'd like ...
Quería (quisiera) ...
Keh-ree'-ah (ke-sye'-rah) ...

Don't bother!
¡No se moleste!
Noh seh mau-les'-teh!

Do you speak English?
¿Habla/hablas inglés?
Ah'-blah/ah'-blahs in-gles'?

I do not speak Spanish
No hablo español
Noh ah'-bloh es-pah-nyaul'

I speak a little Spanish
Hablo un poco de español
Ah'-bloh oon pau'-coh deh es-pah-nyaul'

Do you understand me?
¿Me comprende(s)?
Meh caum-pren'-deh(s)?

I do not understand
No comprendo/entiendo
Noh caum-pren'-doh/en-tyen'-doh

Pardon?
¿Cómo?/¿Perdón?
Cau'-moh?/Per-daun'?

Speak slowly, please
Más despacio, por favor
Mas des-pah'-thyo, paur fah-baur'

Please write it down
¿Puede(s) escribirlo, por favor?
Pweh'-deh(s) es-cre-beer'-loh, paur fah-baur'?

How do you write it?
¿Cómo se escribe?
Cau'-moh seh es-cree'-beh?

Can you spell it, please?
Deletréelo, por favor
Deh-leh-treh'-eh-loh, paur fah-baur'

How do you pronounce it?
¿Cómo se pronuncia?
Cau'-moh seh prau-noon'-thya?

What do you mean?
¿Qué quiere(s) decir?
Keh' kye'-reh(s) deh-theer'?

What does it mean?
¿Qué significa?
Keh' seg-ne-fee'-cah?

How do you say ... in Spanish?
¿Cómo se dice ... en español?
Cau'-moh seh dee'-theh ... en es-pah-nyaul'?

What did you say?
¿Cómo dice(s)?
Cau'-moh dee'-theh(s)?

Could you repeat?
¿Puede(s) repetir?
Pweh'-deh(s) reh-peh-teer'?

ORDERS

Hurry up!	¡Deprisa!	*Deh-pree'-sah!*
Slowly!	¡Despacio!	*Des-pah'-thyo!*
Quickly	¡Rápido!	*Rah'-pe-doh!*
Come on!	¡Venga!	*Ben'-gah!*

Come in!
¡Entre!/¡Adelante!
En'-treh!/Ah-deh-lan'-teh!

Come here!
¡Venga/Ven!
Ben'-gah!/Ben'!

Stop it!
¡Para/pare!
Pah'-rah/pah'-reh!

Be careful!
¡Cuidado!
Kwi-dah'-doh!

Listen!
¡Escuche/escucha!
Es-coo-cheh'/es-coo-chah'!

Give me!
¡Deme/dame!
Deh'-meh/dah'-meh!

Sit down!
¡Siéntese/siéntate!
Syen'-teh-seh/syen'-tah-teh!

Help!
¡Socorro!
Sau-caur'-roh!

Silence
Silencio
Se-len'-thyo

Shut up!
¡Cállese/cállate!
Cah'-lyeh-seh/cah'-lyah-teh!

Let's go!
¡Vamos!
Bah'-mos!

Go away!
¡Vete!
Beh'-teh!

Go ahead!
¡Adelante!
Ah-deh-lan'-teh!

Please be quiet
Por favor, estate quieto
Paur fah-baur', es-tah'-teh kye'-toh

Danger	Peligro	*Peh-lee'-groh*
Beware of ...	Atención al ...	*Ah-ten-thyon' ahl ...*
Caution	Cuidado	*Kwi-dah'-doh*
Private	Privado	*Pre-bah'-doh*
Closed	Cerrado	*Ther-rah'-doh*
Open	Abierto	*Ah-byer'-toh*
Entrance	Entrada	*En-trah'-dah*
Exit	Salida	*Sah-lee'-dah*
Lift	Ascensor	*As-then-saur'*
Out of order	Averiado	*Ah-beh-rya'-doh*
Vacant	Libre	*Lee'-breh*
Engaged	Ocupado	*Au-coo-pah'-doh*
Pull	Tirar	*Te-rar'*
Push	Empujar	*Em-poo-har'*
(Bus) stop	Parada	*Pah-rah'-dah*
Toilets	Servicios	*Ser-bee'-thyos*
Ladies	Señoras	*Seh-nyau'-rahs*
Men	Caballeros	*Cah-bah-lyeh'-rohs*
Exchange	Cambio	*Cahm'-byo*

For sale
Se vende
Seh ben'-deh

For rent (hire)
Se alquila
Seh ahl-kee'-lah

Parking
Aparcamiento
Ah-par-cah-myen'-toh

Self-service
Autoservicio
Ow-tau-ser-bee'-thyo

Keep out
Prohibido el paso
Proy-bee'-doh el pah'-soh

No admittance
Se prohíbe la entrada
Seh proy'-beh lah en-trah'-dah

No smoking
Prohibido fumar
Proy-bee'-doh foo-mar'

Wet paint
Recién pintado
Reh-thyen' pin-tah'-doh

WEATHER

Weather	Tiempo	*Tyem'-poh*
Temperature	Temperatura	*Tem-peh-rah-too'-rah*
Climate	Clima	*Klee'-mah*

Weather forecast
Pronóstico del tiempo
Prau-naus'-te-coh dehl tyem'-poh

What is the weather like?
¿Qué tiempo hace?
Keh' tyem'-poh ah'-theh?

It is hot
Hace calor
Ah'-theh cah-laur'

It is cold
Hace frío
Ah'-theh free'-oh

It is sunny
Hace sol
Ah'-theh saul

It is windy
Hace viento
Ah'-theh byen'-toh

It is cloudy
Está nublado
Es-tah' noo-blah'-doh

It is foggy
Hay niebla
Ah'-y nye'-blah

It is raining
Está lloviendo
Es-tah' lyau-byen'-doh

It is going to rain
Va a llover
Bah ah lyau-ber'

It is still raining
Sigue lloviendo
See'-gheh lyau-byen'-doh

It has stopped raining
Ha dejado de llover
Ah deh-hah'-doh deh lyau-ber'

It is snowing
Está nevando
Es-tah' neh-ban'-doh

It is freezing
Está helando
Es-tah' eh-lan'-doh

The weather is bad
Hace mal tiempo
Ah'-theh mal tyem'-poh

It is a fine day
Hace un tiempo magnífico
*Ah'-theh oon tyem'-poh
mag-nee'-fe-coh*

It is minus six (degrees)
Estamos a seis grados bajo cero
Es-tah'-mos ah seys grah'-dohs bah'-hoh theh'-roh

TIME

Time	Tiempo	*Tyem'-poh*
Hour	Hora	*Au'-rah*
Watch	Reloj	*Reh-lau'*
Minute	Minuto	*Me-noo'-toh*
Second	Segundo	*Seh-goon'-doh*
Half an hour	Media hora	*Meh'-dya au'-rah*
Morning	Mañana	*Mah-nyah'-nah*
Noon	Mediodía	*Meh-dyo-dee'-ah*
Afternoon	Tarde	*Tar'-deh*
Evening	Tarde	*Tar'-deh*
Night	Noche	*Nau'-cheh*
Midnight	Medianoche	*Meh-dya-nau'-cheh*
Day	Día	*Dee'-ah*
Week	Semana	*Seh-mah'-nah*
Month	Mes	*Mehs*
Fortnight	Quincena	*Keen-theh'-nah*

Year	Año	*Ah'-nyoh*
Century	Siglo	*See'-gloh*
Today	Hoy	*Oy*
Yesterday	Ayer	*Ah-yer'*
Tomorrow	Mañana	*Mah-nyah'-nah*
Tonight	Esta noche	*Es'-tah nau-cheh*
Date	Fecha	*Feh'-chah*
Bank Holiday	Día festivo	*Dee'-ah fes-tee'-boh*

What time is it?
¿Qué hora es?
Keh' au'-rah es?

It is seven o'clock
Son las siete
Saun lahs sye'-teh

Ten past seven
Las siete y diez
Lahs sye'-teh ee dyeth'

A quarter past seven
Las siete y cuarto
Lahs sye'-teh ee kwar'-toh

Half past seven
Las siete y media
Lahs sye'-teh ee meh'-dya

A quarter to eight
Las ocho menos cuarto
Lahs au'-choh meh'-nohs kwar'-toh

It is too early/late
Es demasiado temprano/tarde
Es deh-mah-sya'-doh tem-prah'-noh/tar'-deh

Can you tell me the time, please?
¿Puede decirme la hora, por favor?
Pweh'-deh deh-theer'-meh lah au'-rah, paur fah-baur'?

What time does the museum open?
¿A qué hora abre el museo?
Ah keh' au'-rah ah'-breh el moo-seh'-oh?

Days of the week ....

Monday	Lunes	*Loo'-nehs*
Tuesday	Martes	*Mar'-tehs*

Wednesday	Miércoles	*Myer'-cau-lehs*
Thursday	Jueves	*Hweh'-behs*
Friday	Viernes	*Byer'-nehs*
Saturday	Sábado	*Sah'-bah-doh*
Sunday	Domingo	*Dau-meen'-goh*

Months of the year

January	Enero	*Eh-neh'-roh*
February	Febrero	*Feh-breh'-roh*
March	Marzo	*Mar'-thoh*
April	Abril	*Ah-breel'*
May	Mayo	*Mah'-yoh*
June	Junio	*Hoo'-nyo*
July	Julio	*Hoo'-lyo*
August	Agosto	*Ah-gaus'-toh*
September	Septiembre	*Sep-tyem'-breh*
October	Octubre	*Auc-too'-breh*
November	Noviembre	*Nau-byem'-breh*
December	Diciembre	*De-thyem'-breh*

Seasons

Winter	Invierno	*In-byer'-noh*
Spring	Primavera	*Pree-mah-beh'-rah*
Summer	Verano	*Beh-rah'-noh*
Autumn	Otoño	*Au-tau'-nyoh*

Last Sunday
El domingo pasado
El dau-meen'-goh pah-sah'-doh

Next Monday
El lunes próximo
El loo'-nehs prauc'-se-moh

What is the day today?
¿Qué día es hoy?
Keh' dee'-ah es oy?

Today is the first of April
Hoy es uno de abril
Oy es oo'-noh deh ah-breel'

6th November 1954
El seis de noviembre de mil novecientos cincuenta y cuatro
El seys deh nau-byem'-breh deh meel nau-beh-thyen'-tohs thin-kwen'-tah ee kwa'-troh

Christmas
Navidad
Nah-be-dad'

New Year's Day
Año Nuevo
Ah'-nyoh nweh'-boh

Easter (Holy Week)
Semana Santa
Seh-mah'-nah san'-tah

May Day
Primero de Mayo
Pree-meh'-roh deh mah'-yoh

Street, road	Calle	*Cah'-lyeh*
Avenue	Avenida	*Ah-beh-nee'-dah*
Promenade	Paseo	*Pah-seh'-oh*
City centre	Centro	*Then'-troh*
Street corner	Esquina	*Es-kee'-nah*
Suburb (district)	Barrio	*Bar'-ryo*
Outskirts	Afueras	*Ah-fweh'-rahs*
Port (harbour)	Puerto	*Pwer'-toh*
Fountain	Fuente	*Fwehn'-teh*
Square	Plaza	*Plah'-thah*

Bridge	Puente	*Pwehn'-teh*
River	Río	*Ree'-oh*
Garden	Jardín	*Har-deen'*
Park	Parque	*Par'-keh*
Crossroads	Cruce	*Croo'-theh*
Pavement	Acera	*Ah-theh'-rah*
Street light	Farola	*Fah-rau'-lah*
Litter bin	Papelera	*Pah-peh-leh'-rah*
Letter box	Buzón	*Boo-thaun'*
Traffic lights	Semáforo	*Seh-mah'-fau-roh*

Subway
Paso subterráneo
Pah'-soh soob-ter-rah'-neh-oh

Zebra crossing
Paso de cebra
Pah'-soh deh theh'-brah

Traffic policeman
Guardia de tráfico
Gwar'-dya deh trah'-fe-coh

Telephone box
Cabina
Cah-bee'-nah

This way
Por aquí
Paur ah-kee'

That way
Por ahí
Paur ah-y'

Straight on
Todo recto
Tau'-doh rehc'-toh

... metres from here
A ... metros de aquí
Ah ... meh'-trohs deh ah-kee'

To the left
A la izquierda
Ah lah ith-kyer'-dah

To the right
A la derecha
Ah lah deh-reh'-chah

In front
Delante
Deh-lan'-teh

Behind
Detrás
Deh-trahs'

Opposite
Enfrente
En-fren'-teh

Round the corner
Al doblar la esquina
Ahl dau-blar' lah es-kee'-nah

Further on/back
Más adelante/atrás
Mas ah-deh-lan'-teh/ah-tras'

Further up/down
Más arriba/abajo
Mas ar-ree'-bah/ah-bah'-hoh

Excuse me, could you tell me how to get to the bus station?
Perdón, ¿podría decirme por dónde se va a la estación de autobuses?
Per-daun', pau-dree'-ah deh-theer'-meh paur daun'-deh seh bah ah lah es-tah-thyon' deh ow-tau-boo'-sehs?

Excuse me, do you know where the ... is?
Perdón, ¿sabe usted dónde está ...?
Per-daun', sah'-beh oos-ted' daun'-deh es-tah' ...?

I'm sorry, I don't know
Lo siento, no lo sé
Loh syen'-toh, noh loh seh

I'm looking for this address
Estoy buscando esta dirección
Es-toy boos-can'-doh es'-tah de-rec-thyon'

Can you show me on the map?
¿Me lo puede indicar en el mapa?
Meh loh pweh'-deh in-dee-car' en el mah'-pah?

Is it very far?
¿Está muy lejos?
Es-tah' moo'-y leh'-hohs?

How far away is ...?
¿A qué distancia está ...?
Ah keh' dis-tan'-thya es-tah'...?

At the first set of traffic lights, turn right
En el primer semáforo, gire a la derecha
En el pre-mer' seh-mah'-fau-roh, hee'-reh ah lah deh-reh'-chah

Go straight on along this street
Siga por esta misma calle
See'-gah paur es'-tah mees'-mah cah'-lyeh

On the other side of the road
Al otro lado de la calle
Ahl au'-troh lah'-doh deh lah cah'-lyeh

It is the road parallel to this one
Es la paralela a ésta
Es lah pah-rah-leh'-lah ah es'-tah

It is a long way, you'd better take the bus
Está muy lejos, es mejor que tome el autobús
Es-tah' moo'-y leh'-hohs, es meh-haur' keh tau'-meh el ow-tau-boos'

Follow me, I am going in that direction too
Sígame, yo también voy en esa dirección
See'-gah-meh, yoh tam-byen' boy en eh'-sah de-rec-thyon'

It is very difficult to explain
Es muy difícil de explicar
Es moo'-y de-fee'-theel deh ex-ple-car'

PUBLIC BUILDINGS

Hospital	Hospital	*Aus-pe-tahl'*
Post office	Correos	*Caur-reh'-ohs*
Station	Estación	*Es-tah-thyon'*
School	Escuela	*Es-kweh'-lah*
Institute	Instituto	*Ins-te-too'-toh*

University	Universidad	*Oo-ne-ber-se-dad'*
Town Hall	Ayuntamiento	*Ah-yoon-tah-myen-toh*
Court	Juzgado	*Hooth-gah'-doh*
County council	Diputación	*De-poo-tah-teh-aun'*
Embassy	Embajada	*Em-bah-hah'-dah*
Consulate	Consulado	*Caun-soo-lah'-doh*
Police station	Comisaría	*Cau-me-sah-ree'-ah*
Castle	Castillo	*Cas-tee'-lyoh*
Palace	Palacio	*Pah-lah'-thyo*
Church	Iglesia	*E-gleh'-sya*
Cathedral	Catedral	*Cah-teh-drahl'*
Museum	Museo	*Moo-seh'-oh*
Cemetery	Cementerio	*Theh-men-teh'-ryo*

Bullring
Plaza de toros
Plah'-thah deh deh tau'-rohs

Public library
Biblioteca pública
Be-blyo-teh'-cah poo'-ble-cah

Tourist board
Oficina de Turismo
Au-fe-thee'-nah deh too-rees'-moh

AT THE TOURIST INFORMATION CENTRE

We're looking for some accommodation
Estamos buscando alojamiento
Es-tah'-mohs boos-can'-doh ah-lau-hah-myen'-toh

What sort of accommodation are you looking for?
¿Qué clase de alojamiento están buscando?
Keh' clah'-seh deh ah-lau-hah-myen'-toh es-tan' boos-can'-doh?

Do you have a list of youth hostels?
¿Tienen una lista de albergues juveniles?
Tye'-nen oo'-nah lees'-tah deh al-ber'-ghehs hoo-beh-nee'-lehs?

Can you recommend a good restaurant?
¿Podrían recomendarme un buen restaurante?
Pau-dree'-an reh-cau-men-dar'-meh oon bwen res-tow-ran'-teh?

Do you have a map of the city/town?
¿Tienen un plano de la ciudad?
Tye'-nen oon plah'-noh deh lah thew-dad'?

Do you have any brochures on ...?
¿Tienen folletos sobre ...?
Tye'-nen fau-lyeh'-tohs sau'-breh …?

Is there a city tour?
¿Hay visitas guiadas por la ciudad?
Ah'-y be-see'-tahs gheya'-dahs paur lah thew-dad'?

Are there any day trips?
¿Hay viajes organizados de un día?
Ah'-y bya'-hehs aur-gah-nee-thah'-dohs deh oon dee'-ah?

Are there any cultural events on at the moment?
¿Qué eventos culturales hay en la actualidad?
Keh' eh-ben'-tohs cool-too-rah'-lehs ah'-y en lah ac-twa-le-dad'?

Can I book tickets for... here?
¿Podría comprar entradas para ... aquí?
Pau-dree'-ah caum-prar' en-trah'-dahs pah'-rah … ah-kee'?

TRAVELLING

Trip/journey	Viaje	*Bya'-heh*
Destination	Destino	*Des-tee'-noh*
Discount	Descuento	*Des-kwen'-toh*
Offer	Oferta	*Au-fer'-tah*
Flight	Vuelo	*Bweh'-loh*
Reservation	Reserva	*Reh-ser'-bah*
Cancellation	Cancelación	*Can-theh-lah-thyon'*

High/low season
Temporada alta/baja
Tem-pau-rah'-dah al'-tah/bah'-hah

Waiting list
Lista de espera
Lees'-tah deh es-peh'-rah

Travel insurance
Seguro de viaje
Seh-goo'-roh deh bya'-heh

Charter/regular flight
Vuelo chárter/regular
Bweh'-loh charter/reh-goo-lar'

Package tour
Viaje organizado
Bya'-heh aur-gah-nee-thah'-doh

Country retreats
Casas rurales
Cah'-sahs roo-rah'-lehs

Ski resort
Estación de esquí
Es-tah-thyon' deh es-kee'

Theme park
Parque de atracciones
Par'-keh deh ah-trac-thyo'-nehs

Sightseeing
Lugares de interés
Loo-gah'-rehs deh in-teh-rehs'

Daily tours
Excursiones diarias
Ex-coor-syo'-nehs dya'-ryas

Business trip
Viaje de negocios
Bya'-heh deh neh-gau'-thyos

Honeymoon
Viaje de novios
Bya'-heh de nau'-byos

Accommodation	Alojamiento	*Ah-lau-hah-myen'-toh*
Hotel	Hotel	*Au-tehl'*
Guesthouse	Pensión, hostal	*Pen-syon', aus-tahl'*
Hostel	Albergue	*Al-ber'-gheh*

Accommodation with breakfast included
Alojamiento y desayuno
Ah-lau-hah-myen'-toh ee deh-sah-yoo'-noh

We want to take a cruise
Queremos hacer un crucero
Keh-reh'-mos ah-ther' oon croo-theh'-roh

I want to travel all around the country
Quiero hacer un viaje por todo el país
Kye'-roh ah-ther' oon bya'-heh paur tau'-doh el pah-ys'

I'd like to visit the ... region
Desearía visitar la región de ...
Deh-seh-ah-ree'-ah be-se-tar' lah reh-hyon' deh ...

What towns do you advise me to visit?
¿Qué ciudades me aconseja que visite?
Keh' thew-dah'-dehs meh ah-caun-seh'-hah keh be-see'-teh?

I want to go to ... by plane
Quiero ir a ... en avión
Kye'-roh eer ah ... en ah-byon'

It's a three-hour flight
Son tres horas de vuelo
Saun trehs au'-rahs deh bweh'-loh

The plane stops over in ...
El avión hace escala en ...
El ah-byon' ah'-theh es-cah'-lah en ...

What does the flight cost?
¿Cuánto cuesta el vuelo?
Kwan'-toh kwes'-tah el bweh'-loh?

Book me two seats
Resérveme dos plazas
Reh-ser'-beh-meh daus plah'-thahs

How can I get to the airport?
¿Cómo puedo ir al aeropuerto?
Cau'-moh pweh'-doh eer ahl ah-eh-rau-pwer'-toh?

How soon should we be at the airport before take-off?
¿Con qué antelación hay que estar en el aeropuerto?
Caun keh' an-teh-lah-thyon' ah'-y keh es-tar' en el ah-eh-roh-pwer'-toh?

What weight am I allowed?
¿Cuánto peso está permitido?
Kwan'-toh peh'-soh es-tah' per-me-tee'-doh?

I'd like to leave next week
Me gustaría salir la semana próxima
Meh goos-tah-ree'-ah sah-leer' lah seh-mah'-nah prauc'-se-mah

I'd like to stay at four stars hotels
Quisiera alojarme en hoteles de cuatro estrellas
Ke-sye'-rah ah-loh-har'-meh en au-teh'-les deh kwa'-troh es-treh'-lyas

Have you got any tourist brochures?
¿Tienen folletos turísticos?
Tye'-nen oos-ted' fau-lyeh'-tohs too-rees'-te-cos?

Customs	Aduana	*Ah-dwa'-nah*
Documentation	Documentación	*Doh-coo-men-ta-thyon'*
Passport	Pasaporte	*Pah-sah-paur'-teh*
Luggage	Equipaje	*Eh-kee-pah'-heh*
Case (suitcase)	Maleta	*Mah-leh'-tah*
Present (gift)	Regalo	*Reh-gah'-loh*

Handbag
Bolso de mano
Baul'-soh deh mah'-noh

Entry visa
Visado de entrada
Be-sah'-doh deh en-trah'-dah

Passport control
Control de pasaportes
Caun-traul' deh pah-sah-paur'-tes

Customs duties
Derechos de aduana
Deh-reh'-chohs deh ah-dwa'-nah

Nothing to declare
Nada que declarar
Nah'-dah keh deh-clah-rar'

Non-EU citizens
Ciudadanos no comunitarios
*Thew-dah-dah'-nohs noh
cau-moo-ne-tah'-ryos*

Passport, please
Su pasaporte, por favor
Soo pah-sah-paur'-teh, paur fah-baur'

Here you are
Aquí tiene
Ah-kee' tye'-neh

Where have you travelled from?
¿Desde dónde viaja?
Des'-deh daun'-deh bya'-hah?

I'm afraid your passport has expired
Su pasaporte está caducado
Soo pah-sah-paur'-teh es-tah' cah-doo-cah'-doh

What is the purpose of your visit?
¿Cuál es el motivo de su visita?
Kwal' es el mau-tee'-boh deh soo be-see'-tah?

Holidays, touring, family affairs, studies
Vacaciones, turismo, asuntos familiares, estudios
Bah-cah-thyo'-nes, too-rees'-moh, ah-soon'-tohs fah-me-lya'-rehs, es-too'-dyos

How long will you be staying?
¿Cuánto tiempo va a permanecer aquí?
Kwan'-toh tyem'-poh bah ah per-mah-neh-ther' ah-kee'?

Where will you be staying?
¿Dónde va a alojarse?
Daun'-deh bah ah ah-lau-har'-seh?

You have to fill in this immigration form
Debe rellenar este formulario de inmigración
Deh'-beh reh-lye-nar' es'-teh faur-moo-lah'-ryo deh inmi-grah-thyon'

Have you got anything to declare?
¿Tiene usted algo que declarar?
Tye'-neh oos-ted' al'-goh keh deh-clah-rar'?

Could you open this bag/this suitcase, please?
¿Podría abrir esa bolsa/esa maleta, por favor?
Pau-dree'-ah ah-breer' eh'-sah baul'-sah/eh'-sah mah-leh'-tah, paur fah-baur'?

I only have personal effects

Sólo llevo objetos de uso personal

Sau'-loh lyeh'-boh aub-heh'-tohs deh oo'-soh per-sau-nal'

You have to pay duty on these items

Debe pagar recargo por estos objetos

Deh'-beh pah-gar' reh-car'-goh paur es'-tohs aub-heh'-tohs

Is everything OK?

¿Está todo en orden?

Es-tah' tau'-doh en aur'-den?

Where is the exchange office?

¿Dónde está la oficina de cambio?

Daun'-deh es-tah' lah au-fe-thee'-nah deh cam'-byo?

What is the rate for the euro/pound/dollar?

¿Cuál es la cotización del euro/libra/dólar?

Kwal' es lah cau-te-tha-thyon' dehl eh'-oo-roh/lee'-brah/dau'-lar?

Can you change me ... into euros?

¿Puede cambiarme ... en euros?

Pweh'-deh cahm-be-ar'-meh ... en eh'-oo-rohs?

Where is a taxi rank/a bus stop?

¿Dónde hay una parada de taxis/de autobuses?

Daun'-deh ah'-y oo'-nah pah-rah'-dah deh tac'-ses/ow-tau-boo'-sehs?

AT THE AIRPORT

Airport	Aeropuerto	*Ah-eh-rau-pwer'-toh*
Plane	Avión	*Ah-byon'*
Flight	Vuelo	*Bweh'-loh*
Stopover	Escala	*Es-cah'-lah*
Passenger	Pasajero	*Pah-sah-heh'-roh*
Timetable	Horario	*Au-rah'-ryo*
Check-in desk	Facturación	*Fac-too-rah-thyon'*
Ticket	Billete	*Be-lyeh'-teh*
Arrivals	Llegadas	*Lyeh-gah'-dahs*
Departures	Salidas	*Sah-lee'-dahs*

Airlines
Líneas aéreas
Lee'-neh-ahs ah-eh'-reh-ahs

Airline counter
Mostrador
Maus-trah-daur'

International/domestic flight
Vuelo nacional/internacional
*Bweh'-loh nah-thyo-nahl'/
in-ter-nah-thyo-nahl'*

Non-stop flight
Vuelo directo
Bweh'-loh de-rec'-toh

Can I see your ticket, please?
¿Me enseña su billete, por favor?
Meh en-seh'-nyah soo be-lyeh'-teh, paur fah-baur'?

Do you have your passport with you?
Su pasaporte, por favor
Soo pah-sah-paur'-teh, paur fah-baur'

How many bags are you checking?
¿Qué equipaje va a facturar?
Keh' eh-ke-pah'-heh bah ah fac-too-rar'?

Will you be bringing a carry-on luggage?
¿Llevará equipaje de mano?
Lyeh-bah-rah' eh-ke-pah'-heh deh mah'-noh?

You are going to have to pay the overweight
Tendrá que pagar por exceso de equipaje
Ten-drah' keh pah-ga' paur ex-theh'-soh deh eh-ke-pah'-heh

Do you need any tags for your luggage?
¿Necesita etiquetas para su equipaje?
Neh-theh-see'-tah eh-te-keh'-tahs pah'-rah soo eh-ke-pah'-heh?

Would you like an aisle or a window seat?
¿Pasillo o ventanilla?
Pah-see'-lyoh oh ben-tah-nee'-lyah?

You'll board at gate …
Debe embarcar por la puerta …
Deh'-beh em-bar-car' paur lah pwer'-tah …

Please be at the gate thirty minutes before your flight
Debe estar en la puerta de embarque treinta minutos antes
Deh'-beh es-tar' en lah pwer'-tah deh em-bar'-keh treyn-tah me-noo'-tohs an'-tes

What time does flight … for … leave?
¿A qué hora sale el vuelo … para …?
Ah keh' au'-rah sah'-leh el bweh'-loh … pah'-rah …?

Your flight is expected to take off on time
Su vuelo saldrá a la hora prevista
Soo bweh'-loh sahl-drah' ah lah au'-rah preh-bees'-tah

Your flight has been delayed by two hours
Su vuelo tiene un retraso de dos horas
Soo bweh'-loh tye'-neh oon reh-trah'-soh deh daus au'-rahs

Flight ... to ... has been cancelled
El vuelo ... con destino a ... ha sido cancelado
El bweh'-loh caun des-tee'-noh ah ... ah see'-doh can-theh-lah'-doh

Where can I get a luggage trolley/a wheelchair?
¿Dónde puedo conseguir un carrito/una silla de ruedas?
Daun'-deh pweh'-doh caun-seh-gheer' oon cah-rree'-toh/oo'-nah see'-lyah deh rweh'-dahs

Passport control	Metal detector
Control de pasaportes	Detector de metales
Caun-traul' deh pah-sah-paur'-tes	*Deh-tec-taur' deh meh-tah'-lehs*

Could I see your passport and boarding card, please?
Por favor, su pasaporte y su tarjeta de embarque
Paur fah-baur', soo pah-sah-paur'-teh ee soo tar-heh'-tah deh em-bar'-keh

Could you put any metallic objects into the tray, please?
Ponga todos los objetos metálicos en la cesta, por favor
Paun'-gah tau'-dohs lohs aub-heh'-tohs meh-tah'-lee-cohs en lah thehs'-tah, paur fah-baur'

Do you have any liquids or sharp objects in your hand luggage?
¿Lleva algún líquido u objeto punzante en su equipaje de mano?
Lyeh'-ba al-goon' lee'-ke-doh oo aub-heh'-toh poon-than'-teh en soo eh-ke-pah'-heh deh mah'-noh?

Could you take off your belt, please?
¿Podría quitarse el cinturón, por favor?
Pau-dree'-ah kee-tar'-seh el thin-too-raun', paur fah-baur'?

Departures lounge
Sala de espera
Sah'-lah deh es-peh'-rah

Gate
Puerta de embarque
Pwer'-tah deh em-bar'-keh

Duty free shopping
Tienda libre de impuestos
Tyen'-dah lee'-breh deh im-pwes'-tohs

The flight to ... (from ...)
El vuelo con destino a ... (procedente de ...)
El bweh'-loh caun des-tee'-noh ah ... (prau-theh-den'-teh deh ...)

I'm looking for the ... terminal
Busco la terminal ...
Boos'-coh la ter-mee-nahl' ...

Passengers for flight ... should go to gate ...
Se ruega a los pasajeros del vuelo ... embarquen por la puerta ...
Seh rweh'-gah ah lohs pah-sah-heh'-ros dehl bweh'-loh ... em-bar'-ken paur lah pwer'-tah ...

This is the final boarding call for passengers booked on flight ...
Última llamada para los pasajeros del vuelo ...
Ool'-te-mah lyah-mah'-dah pah'-rah lohs pah-sah-heh'-ros dehl bweh'-loh ...

DURING THE FLIGHT

Seat   Asiento   *Ah-syen'-toh*

First class
Primera clase
Pre-meh'-rah clah'-seh

Economy class
Clase turista
Clah'-seh too-rees'-tah

What's your seat number, please?
¿Cuál es el número de su asiento, por favor?
Kwal' es el noo'-meh-roh deh soo ah-syen'-toh, paur fah-baur'?

Could you please put that in the overhead locker?
¿Podría colocar eso en el compartimento superior?
Pau-dree'-ah cau-lau-car' eh'-soh en el caum-par-te-men'-toh
soo-peh-ryor'?

Pilot	Piloto	*Pe-lau'-toh*
Stewardess	Azafata	*Ah-thah-fah'-tah*
Window	Ventanilla	*Ben-tah-nee'-lyah*
Crew	Tripulación	*Tre-poo-lah-thyon'*
Take-off	Despegue	*Des-peh'-gheh*
Landing	Aterrizaje	*Ah-ter-re-thah'-heh*
Lavatory	Servicios	*Ser-bee'-thyos*
Life jacket	Chaleco salvavidas	*Chah-leh'-coh*
		sal-bah-bee'-dahs

Please fasten your seatbelt and return your seat to the upright position
Por favor, abróchense los cinturones y pongan sus asientos en posición vertical
Paur fah-baur', ah-brau'-chen-seh lohs thin-too-rau'-nehs ee paun'-gan
soos ah-syen'-tohs en pau-se-thyon' ber-tee-cahl'

Please turn off all mobile phones and electronic devices
Por favor, apaguen sus teléfonos móviles y demás aparatos electrónicos
Paur fah-baur', ah-pah'-ghen soos teh-leh'-fau-nohs mau'-be-lehs ee
deh-mas' ah-pah-rah'-tohs eh-lec-trau'-nee-cohs

Smoking is prohibited for the duration of the flight
Está prohibido fumar durante todo el vuelo
Es-tah' proy-bee'-doh foo-mar' doo-ran'-teh tau'-doh el bweh'-loh

Motion sickness	Mareo	*Mah-reh-oh*
Turbulence	Turbulencia	*Toor-boo-len'-thya*

Meal tray
Bandeja de comida
Ban-deh'-hah deh cau-mee'-dah

Vegetarian meal
Comida vegetariana
Cau-me'-dah beh-heh-ta-rya'-nah

We shall land in ten minutes

Tomaremos tierra dentro de diez minutos

Tau-mah-reh-mohs tyer'-rah den'-troh de dyeth' me-noo'-tohs

Please stay in your seat until the aircraft has come to a complete standstill

Por favor, permanezcan en sus asientos hasta que el aparato se haya inmovilizado totalmente

Paur fah-baur', por mah neth'-can en soos ah-syen'-tohs as'-tah keh el ah-pah-rah'-toh seh ah'-yah in-mau-be-lc-thah'-doh tau-tahl'-men-teh

Pick up your luggage at the terminal

Recojan su equipaje en la terminal

Reh-cau'-han soo eh-ke-pah'-heh en lah ter-me-nahl'

One of my suitcases has been lost

Se me ha perdido una maleta

Seh meh ah per-dee'-doh oo'-nah mah-leh'-tah

Where can I report it?

¿Dónde puedo reclamar?

Daun'-deh pweh'-doh reh-clah-mar'?

Lost property

Objetos perdidos

Aub-heh'-tohs per-dee'-dohs

Fill in this claim form

Rellene esta hoja de reclamaciones

Reh-lyeh'-neh es'-tah au'-hah deh reh-clah-mah-thyo'-nehs

Train	Tren	*Tren*
Station	Estación	*Es-tah-thyon'*
Platform	Andén	*An-den'*
Track	Vía	*Bee'-ah*
Carriage	Vagón	*Bah-gaun'*
Sleeper	Litera	*Le-teh'-rah*
Compartment	Compartimento	*Caum-par-te-men'-toh*
Passenger	Viajero	*Bya-heh'-roh*
Inspector	Revisor	*Reh-be-saur'*
Bag	Bolsa	*Baul'-sah*
Rucksack	Mochila	*Mau-chee'-lah*
Briefcase	Maletín	*Mah-leh-teen'*

Single (return) ticket
Billete de ida (de ida y vuelta)
*Be-lyeh'-teh deh ee'-dah
(deh ee'-dah ee bwel'-tah)*

Ticket office
Despacho de billetes
Des-pah'-choh deh be-lyeh'-tehs

First class
Primera clase
Pre-meh'-rah clah'-seh

Coach class
Clase turista
Clah'-seh too-rees'-tah

Sleeping car
Coche-cama
Cau'-cheh cah'-mah

Timetable
Cuadro de horarios
Kwa'-droh deh au-rah'-ryos

Left-luggage office
Consigna
Caun-seeg'-nah

Lost property
Objetos perdidos
Aub-heh'-tohs per-dee'-dohs

High-speed train, local train
AVE, tren de cercanías
Ah'-beh, trehn deh ther-cah-nee'-as

At which ticket office do I get a ticket to ...?

¿En qué ventanilla despachan los billetes para ...?

En keh' ben-tah-nee'-lyah des-pah'-chan lohs be-lyeh'-tehs pah'-rah ...?

Where are the ticket machines?

¿Dónde están las máquinas expendedoras de billetes?

Daun'-deh es-tan' lahs mah'-kee-nahs ex-pen-deh-dau'-rahs deh be-lyeh' toho?

What time is the last train to ...?

¿A qué hora sale el último tren para ...?

Ah keh' au'-rah sah'-leh el ool'-te-moh trehn pah'-rah ...?

How much does a return ticket to ... cost?

¿Cuánto cuesta un billete de ida y vuelta a ...?

Kwan'-toh kwes'-tah oon be-lyeh'-teh deh ee'-dah ee bwel'-tah ah ...?

Is there a half price ticket for students/children/senior citizens?

¿Hay descuentos para estudiantes/niños/pensionistas?

Ah'-y des-kwen'-tohs pah'-rah es-too-de-an'-tes/nee'-nyohs/pen-syo-nees'-tahs?

When will you be coming back?

¿Para cuándo quiere la vuelta?

Pah'-rah kwan'-doh kye'-reh lah bwel'-tah?

Is there a train to ...?	**Two tickets to ...**
¿Hay un tren para ...?	Dos billetes para ...
Ah'-y oon trehn pah'-rah ...?	*Daus be-lyeh'-tehs pah'-rah ...*

What time does the train to ... leave?

¿A qué hora sale el tren para ...?

Ah keh' au'-rah sah'-leh el trehn pah'-rah ...?

Can I have a timetable, please?

¿Me da un horario, por favor?

Meh dah oon au-rah'-ryo, paur fah-baur'?

Which platform do I need for ...?
¿De qué andén sale el tren para ...?
Deh keh' an-den' sah'-leh el trehn pah'-rah ...?

The next train to ... will depart from platform ...
El tren con destino a ... saldrá del andén ...
El trehn caun des-tee'-noh ah ... sal-drah' dehl an-den' ...

Do I have to change trains?
¿Tengo que hacer transbordo?
Ten'-goh keh ah-ther' trans-baur'-doh?

Does this train stop at ...?
¿Para este tren en ...?
Pah'-rah es'-teh trehn en ...?

What time does it arrive at ...?
¿A qué hora llega a ...?
Ah keh' au'-rah lyeh'-gah ah ...?

Is this seat vacant/taken?
¿Está libre/ocupado este asiento?
Es-tah' lee'-breh/au-coo-pah'-doh es'-teh ah-syen'-toh?

Which station is next?
¿Cuál es la próxima estación?
Kwal' es lah prauc'-se-mah es-tah-thyon'?

Is there a buffet car on the train?
¿Hay vagón-restaurante en este tren?
Ah'-y bah-gaun' res-tow-ran'-teh en es'-teh trehn?

Car	Coche	*Cau'-cheh*
Coach	Autocar	*Ow-tau-car'*
Lorry	Camión	*Cah-myon'*
Bus	Autobús	*Ow-tau-boos'*
Van	Furgoneta	*Foor-gau-neh'-tah*
Motorcycle	Moto	*Mau'-toh*
Road	Carretera	*Car-reh-teh'-rah*
Motorway	Autopista	*Ow-tau-pees'-tah*
Dual carriage way	Autovía	*Ow-tau-bee'-ah*
Toll	Peaje	*Peh-ah'-heh*
Crossroads	Cruce	*Croo'-theh*
Main road	Carretera Nacional	*Car-reh-teh'-rah nah-thyo-nahl'*

Rest area
Área de descanso
Ah'-reh-ah deh des-can'-soh

Services
Área de servicio
Ah'-reh-ah deh ser-bee'-thyo

Speed limit
Límite de velocidad
Lee'-me-teh deh beh-lau-the-dad'

Driving licence
Permiso de conducir
Per-mee'-soh deh caun-doo-theer'

Level crossing
Paso a nivel
Pah'-soh ah ne-bel'

Dangerous bend
Curva peligrosa
Coor'-bah peh-le-grau'-sah

U-turn
Cambio de sentido
Cahm'-byo deh sen-tee'-doh

Diversion
Desviación
Des-bya-thyon'

One-way street
Dirección única
De-rec-thyon' oo'-ne-cah

Dead end
Calle sin salida
Cah'-lyeh sin sah-lee'-dah

Pedestrian crossing
Paso de peatones
Pah'-soh deh peh-ah-tau'-nehs

Road sign
Señal de tráfico
Seh-nyahl' deh trah'-fe-coh

Roadworks
Obras
Au'-brahs

No through road
Calle cortada
Cah'-lyeh caur-tah'-dah

Traffic delay
Retención
Reh-ten-thyon'

Slow down
Modere su velocidad
Moh-deh'-reh soo beh-lau-the-dad'

No overtaking
Prohibido adelantar
Proy-bee'-doh ah-deh-lan-tar'

No stopping
Prohibido detenerse
Proy-bee'-doh deh-teh-ner'-seh

Traffic lights
Semáforo
Seh-mah'-fau-roh

Parking
Aparcamiento
Ah-par-cah-myen'-toh

Give way
Ceda el paso
Theh'-dah el pah'-soh

Bus lane
Carril bus
Car-reel' boos

Breath alcohol test
Control de alcoholemia
*Caun-traul' deh
al-cau-au-leh'-myah*

Speed cameras
Velocidad controlada por radar
*Beh-lau-the-dad' caun-trau-lah'-
dah paur rah-dar'*

The road to ..., please

Para ir a ..., por favor

Pah'-rah eer ah ..., paur fah-baur'

Is this the way to ...?

¿Es ésta la carretera para ...?

Es es'-tah lah car-reh-teh'-rah pah'-rah ...?

How far is ...?

¿A qué distancia está ...?

Ah keh' dis-tan'-thya es-tah' ...?

It is not far. There are some ... kilometres

No está lejos. Hay unos ... kilómetros

Noh es-tah' leh'-hohs. Ah'-y oo'-nohs ... ki-lau'-meh-trohs

Is the road good?	**There are many bends**
¿Es buena la carretera?	Hay muchas curvas
Es bweh'-nah lah car-reh-teh'-rah?	*Ah'-y moo'-chahs coor'-bahs*

Where can I buy a road map?

¿Dónde puedo comprar un mapa de carreteras?

Daun'-deh pweh'-doh caum-prar' oon mah'-pah deh car-reh-teh'-ras?

Which is the best road to get to the coast?

¿Cuál es la mejor carretera para ir a la costa?

Kwal' es lah meh-haur' car-reh-teh'-rah pah'-rah eer ah lah caus'-tah?

Excuse me, is this the turn off for ...?

Disculpe, ¿cuál es la salida para ...?

Dis-cool'-peh, kwal' es lah sah-lee'-dah pah'-rah ...?

Can I park here?	**There is no parking place**
¿Puedo aparcar aquí?	No hay aparcamiento
Pweh'-doh ah-par-car' ah-kee'?	*Noh ah'-y ah-par-cah-myen'-toh*

CAR HIRE

I'd like to hire a car
Quisiera alquilar un coche
Ke-sye'-rah al-ke-lar' oon cau'-cheh

What type of car do you want, manual or automatic?
¿Qué tipo de coche desea, manual o automático?
*Keh' tee'-poh deh cau'-cheh deh-seh'-ah, mah-nwal' oh
ow-tau-mah'-te-coh?*

What is the cost per km/per day?
¿Cuál es el precio por kilómetro/por día?
Kwal' es el preh'-thyo paur ki-lau'-meh-troh/paur dee'-ah?

... euros a day with unlimited mileage, plus VAT
... euros al día sin límite de kilometraje, más IVA
*... eh'-oo-rohs ahl dee'-ah sin lee'-me-teh deh ki-lau-meh-trah'-heh,
mas ee'-bah*

Insurance included
Seguro incluido
Seh-goo'-roh in-clwi'-doh

For how many days?
¿Cuántos días?
Kwan'-tohs dee'-ahs?

Does it take petrol or diesel?
¿Es diésel o gasolina?
Es dye'-sel oh gah-sau-lee'-nah?

Must I leave a deposit?
¿Tengo que dejar un depósito?
Ten'-goh keh deh-har' oon deh-pau'-se-toh?

Has this car got central locking/air conditioning/a CD player?
¿Tiene el coche cierre centralizado/aire acondicionado/reproductor de CDs?
Tye'-neh el cau'-cheh thyer'-reh then-trah-le-thah'-doh/ah'-e-reh ah-caun-de-thyo-nah'-doh/reh-prau-dooc-taur' deh theh-dehs'?

Can I pay with a credit card?
¿Puedo pagar con tarjeta?
Pweh'-doh pah-gar' caun tar-heh'-tah?

Could I see your driving licence?
¿Puedo ver su carné de conducir?
Pweh'-doh ber soo car-neh' deh caun-doo-theer'?

You have to bring it back with a full tank
Tiene que devolverlo con el depósito lleno
Tye'-neh keh deh-baul-ber'-loh caun el deh-pau'-se-toh lyeh'-noh

How do you open the bonnet/the boot/the petrol tank?
¿Cómo se abre el capó/el maletero/el depósito de combustible?
Cau'-moh seh ah'-breh cah-poh'/el deh-poh'-se-toh deh caum-boos-tee'-bleh?

AT A PETROL STATION

Petrol station	Gasolinera	*Gah-sau-le-neh'-rah*
Petrol	Gasolina	*Gah-sau-lee'-nah*
Diesel	Diésel	*Dye'-sel*
Air	Aire	*Ah'-y-reh*
Oil	Aceite	*Ah-they'-teh*
Water	Agua	*Ah'-gwa*
Tank	Depósito	*Deh-pau'-se-toh*

| Car wash | Túnel de lavado | *Too'-nehl deh* |
| | | *lah-bah'doh* |

Antifreeze	**Brake fluid**
Anticongelante	Líquido de frenos
An-te-caun-heh-lan'-teh	*Lee'-ke-doh deh freh'-nohs*

How far is it to the next services?
¿A qué distancia está la próxima área de servicio?
Ah keh' dis-tan'-thya es-tah' lah prauc'-se-mah ah'-reh-ah deh ser-bee'-thyo?

Is there a petrol station near here?
¿Hay una gasolinera cerca de aquí?
Ah'-y oo'-nah gah-sau-le-neh'-rah ther'-cah deh ah-kee'?

Put in twenty liters of petrol, please
Veinte litros de gasolina, por favor
Beh'-in-teh lee'-trohs deh gah-sau-lee'-nah, paur fah-aur'

Fill the tank, please	**How much is it?**
Lleno, por favor	¿Cuánto es?
Lyeh'-noh, paur fah-baur'	*Kwan'-toh es?*

Can I check my tyre pressure here?
¿Puedo mirar la presión de mis neumáticos aquí?
Pwe'-doh me-rar' lah preh-syon' deh mees neh-oo-mah'-te-cos ah-kee'?

Please, give me a bottle of oil
Deme una botella de aceite, por favor
Deh'-meh oo'-nah boh-teh'-lyah deh ah-they-teh, paur fah-baur'

How long will it take to wash it?
¿Cuánto tardarán en lavarlo?
Kwan'-toh tar-dah-ran' en lah-bar'-loh?

Where are the toilets, please?
¿Dónde están los servicios, por favor?
Daun'-deh es-tan' lohs ser-bee'-thyos, paur fah-baur'?

AT A REPAIR SHOP

Repair shop	Taller	*Tah-lyer'*
Mechanic	Mecánico	*Meh-cah'-ne-coh*
Breakdown	Avería	*Ah-beh-ree'-ah*
Puncture	Pinchazo	*Pen-chah'-thoh*
Number-plate	Matrícula	*Mah-tree'-coo-lah*
Wing mirror	Retrovisor	*Re-trau-be-saur'*
Headlight	Faro	*Fah'-roh*
Indicator	Intermitente	*In-ter-me-ten'-teh*
Rear-light	Piloto	*Pe-lau'-toh*
Bonnet	Capó	*Cah-pauh'*
Boot	Maletero	*Mah-leh-teh'-roh*
Door	Puerta	*Pwer'-tah*
Windscreen	Parabrisas	*Pah-rah-bree'-sahs*
Window	Ventanilla	*Ben-tah-nee'-lyah*
Bumper	Parachoques	*Pah-rah-chau'-kehs*
Wheel	Rueda	*Rweh'-dah*
Tyre	Neumático	*Neh-oo-mah'-te-coh*
Shock absorber	Amortiguador	*Ah-maur-te-gwa-daur'*
Motor	Engine	*Mau-taur'*
Starter motor	Estárter	*Es-tar'-ter*

Carburettor	Carburador	*Car-boo-rah-daur'*
Alternator	Alternador	*Al-ter-nah-daur'*
Mudguard	Guardabarros	*Gwar-dah-bar'-rohs*
Coil	Bobina	*Bau-bee'-nah*
Battery	Batería	*Bah-teh-ree'-ah*
Spark plug	Bujía	*Boo-hee'-ah*
Fuse	Fusible	*Foo-see'-bleh*
Piston	Pistón	*Pees-taun'*
Connecting rod	Biela	*Bye'-lah*
Crankcase	Cárter	*Car'-ter*
Crankshaft	Cigüeñal	*The-gweh-nyahl'*
Radiator	Radiador	*Rah-dya-daur'*
Jack	Gato	*Gah'-toh*
Cylinder head	Culata	*Coo-lah'-tah*
Set of tools	Herramientas	*Er-rah-myen'-tahs*
Clutch	Embrague	*Em-brah'-gheh*
Steering-wheel	Volante	*Boh-lan'-teh*
Accelerator pedal	Acelerador	*Ah-theh-leh-rah-daur'*

Spare wheel
Rueda de repuesto
Rweh'-dah deh reh-pwes'-toh

Exhaust-pipe
Tubo de escape
Too'-boh deh es-cah'-peh

Cylinder head joint
Junta de culata
Hoon'-tah deh coo-lah'-tah

Fan belt
Correa del ventilador
Caur-reh'-ah dehl ben-te-lah-daur'

Spare parts
Piezas de repuesto
Pye'-thas deh reh-pwes'-toh

Air/oil filter
Filtro de aire/aceite
*Feel'-troh deh ah'-e-reh/
ah-the'y-teh*

Gearbox
Caja de cambio
Cah'-hah deh cahm'-byo

Ignition key
Llave de contacto
Lyah'-beh deh caun-tac'-toh

Gear lever
Palanca de cambio
Pah-lan'-cah deh cahm'-byo

Reverse
Marcha atrás
Mar'-chah ah-trahs'

Footbrake
Pedal de freno
Peh-dahl' deh freh'-noh

Handbrake
Freno de mano
Freh'-noh deh mah'-noh

First, second, third gear
Primera, segunda, tercera (marcha)
Pre-meh'-rah, seh-goon'-dah, ter-theh'-rah (mar'-chah)

Where is a repair shop?
¿Dónde hay un taller?
Daun'-deh ah'-y oon tah-lyer'?

My car has broken down ... kilometres from here
Mi coche se ha averiado a ... kilómetros de aquí
Mee cau'-cheh seh ah ah-beh-rya'-doh ah ... ki-lau'-meh-trohs deh ah-kee'

Can you tow my car?
¿Pueden remolcar mi coche?
Pweh'-den reh-maul-car' mee cau'-cheh?

What is the matter?
¿Qué le pasa?
Keh' leh pah'-sah?

There's a strange noise
Se oye un ruido extraño
Seh au'-yeh oon rwi'-doh ex-trah'-nyoh

There is something wrong with the steering/the brakes
Algo va mal con la dirección asistida/los frenos
Al'-goh bah mahl caun lah de-rec-thyon' ah-sis-tee'-dah/lohs freh'-nohs

I've got a puncture
He tenido un pinchazo
Eh teh-nee'-doh oon pin-chah'-thoh

I've got a flat tyre
Se ha desinflado una rueda
Seh ah deh-sin-flah'-doh oo'-nah rweh'-dah

The car is losing oil
El coche está perdiendo aceite
El cau'-cheh es-tah' per-dyen'-doh ah-they-teh

The battery is flat
La batería está descargada
Lah bah-teh-ree'-ah es-tah' des-car-gah'-dah

The clutch does not work
No funciona el embrague
Noh foon-thyo'-nah el em-brah'-gheh

The fan belt is broken
La correa del ventilador está rota
Lah caur-reh'-ah dehl ben-te-lah-daur' es-tah' rau'-tah

Check the brakes
Revise los frenos
Reh-bee'-seh lohs freh'-nohs

The fuses are burned
Se han fundido los fusibles
Seh an foon-dee'-doh lohs foo-see'-blehs

The engine won't start
El motor no arranca
El mau-taur' noh ar-ran'-cah

The radiator leaks
El radiador pierde líquido
El rah-dya-daur' pyer'-deh

Can you repair it temporarily?
¿Pueden hacer un arreglo provisional?
Pweh'-den ah-ther' oon ar-reh'-gloh prau-be-syo-nahl'?

How long will it take to repair it?
¿Cuánto tardarán en arreglarlo?
Kwan'-toh tar-dah-ran' en ar-reh-glar'-loh?

Please, repair it as soon as possible
Por favor, repárelo lo antes posible
Paur fah-baur', reh-pah'-reh-loh lau an'-tes pau-see'-bleh

We have to send for spare parts
Tenemos que pedir repuestos
Teh-neh'-mohs keh peh-deer' reh-pwes'-tohs

It is already repaired
Ya está arreglado
Yah es-tah' ar-reh-glah'-doh

I need a receipt
¿Me puede hacer una factura?
Meh pweh'-deh ah-ther' oo'-nah fac-too'-rah?

ACCIDENTS

Crash	Choque	*Chau'-keh*
Injured	Herido	*Eh-ree'-doh*
Dead	Muerto	*Mwer'-toh*
Tow truck	Grúa	*Groo'-ah*

Help point
Puesto de socorro
Pwes'-toh deh sau-caur'-roh

Accident report
Parte de accidente
Par'-teh deh ac-the-den'-teh

Reflective jacket
Chaleco reflectante
Chah-leh'-coh reh-flec-than'-teh

Third party policy
Seguro a terceros
Seh-goo'-roh ah ter-theh'-rohs

Comprehensive policy
Seguro a todo riesgo
Seh-goo'-roh ah tau'-doh ryes'-goh

Warning triangle
Triángulo de señalización
Te-an'-goo-loh deh seh-nyah-le-thah-thyon'

Can you help me?
¿Puede usted ayudarme?
Pweh'-deh oos-ted' ah-yoo-dar'-meh?

There has been an accident ... kilometres from here
Ha habido un accidente a ... kilómetros de aquí
Ah ah-bee'-doh oon ac-the-den'-teh ah ... ki-lau'-meh-trohs deh ah-kee'

Where is the nearest hospital?
¿Dónde está el hospital más próximo?
Daun'-deh es-tah' el aus-pe-tahl' mas prauc'-se-moh?

Please, call an ambulance
Por favor, llamen a una ambulancia
Paur fah-baur', lyah'-men ah oo'-nah am-boo-lan'-thya

Is there someone injured?
¿Hay algún herido?
Ah'-y al-goon' eh-ree'-doh?

Here is my insurance cover (the car documents)
Aquí está mi póliza de seguros (los papeles del coche)
Ah-kee' es-tah' mee pau'-le-thah deh seh-goo'-rohs (lohs pah-peh'-lehs dehl cau'-cheh)

Could I see your driving licence?
¿Podría ver su carné de conducir?
Pau-dree'-ah ber soo car-neh' deh caun-doo-theer'?

I had right of way
Yo tenía preferencia
Yoh teh-nee'-ah preh-feh-ren'-thya

It was your fault
Fue culpa suya
Fweh' cool'-pah soo-yah

Do you know what speed you were doing?

¿Sabe usted a qué velocidad iba conduciendo?

Sah'-beh oos-ted' ah keh' beh-lau-the-dad' ee'-bah
caun-doo-thyen'-doh?

Could you blow into this tube, please?

¿Podría soplar en este tubo, por favor?

Pau-dree'-ah sau-plar' en es'-teh too'-boh, paur fah-baur'?

Your alcohol level is over the limit

Su tasa de alcohol es superior a la permitida

Soo tah'-sah deh al-cau-aul' es soo-peh-ryor' ah lah per-me-tee'-dah

Come with me to the police station

Acompáñeme a la comisaría

Ah-caum-pah'-nyeh-meh ah lah cau-me-sah-ree'-ah

TRAVELLING BY BOAT

Port	Puerto	*Pwer'-toh*
Quay (dock)	Muelle	*Mweh'-lyeh*
Ship	Barco	*Bar'-coh*
Yacht	Yate	*Yah'-teh*
Ferry	Transbordador	*Trans-baur-dah-daur'*
Cruise ship	Transatlántico	*Trans-at-lan'-te-coh*
Shipping company	Compañía marítima	*Caum-pah-nyee'-ah* *mah-reeh'-te-mah*

Deck	Cubierta	*Coo-byer'-tah*
Deckchair	Hamaca	*Ah-mah'-cah*
Cabin	Camarote	*Cah-mah-rau'-teh*
Hold	Bodega	*Bau-deh'-gah*
Captain	Capitán	*Cah-pe-tan'*
Steward	Camarero	*Cah-mah-reh'-roh*
Sailor	Marinero	*Mah-re-neh'-roh*
Lifejacket	Chaleco salvavidas	*Chah-leh'-coh*
		sal-bah-bee'-dahs

To heave up anchor
Levar anclas
Leh-bar' an'-clas

To come alongside
Atracar
Ah-trah-car'

To call (at a port)
Hacer escala
Ah-ther' es-cah'-lah

Which way is it to the port?
¿Por dónde se va al puerto?
Paur daun'-deh seh bah ahl poo-er'-toh?

What time is the next boat to ...?
¿A qué hora sale el próximo barco a ...?
Ah keh' au'-rah sah'-leh el prauc'-se-moh bar'-coh ah ...?

I'd like a two-berth cabin/a deck passenger ticket
Quisiera un camarote de dos camas/un pasaje de cubierta
Ke-sye'-rah reh-ser-bar' oon cah-mah-rau'-teh deh daus cah'-mas/
oon pah-sah'-heh deh coo-byer'-tah

I'd like a ticket for a car and two passengers
Por favor, un billete para un coche y dos pasajeros
Paur fah-baur', oon be-lyeh'-teh pah'-rah oon cau'-cheh ee daus
pah-sah-heh'-ros

How soon before the departure time do I have to arrive?

¿Con qué antelación tengo que llegar antes de la salida?

Caun keh' an-teh-lah-thyon' ten'-goh keh lyeh-gar' an'-tes deh lah sah-lee'-dah?

How long is the crossing?

¿Cuánto dura la travesía?

Kwan'-toh doo'-rah lah trah-beh-see'-ah?

Which quay does the ship sail from?

¿De qué muelle sale el barco?

Deh keh' mweh'-lyeh sah'-leh el bar'-coh?

Where is cabin number ...?

Disculpe, ¿dónde está el camarote número ...?

Dis-cool'-peh, daun'-deh es-tah' el cah-mah-rau'-teh noo'-meh-roh...?

I feel seasick. Have you got anything for seasickness?

Estoy mareado. ¿Tiene usted algo contra el mareo?

Es-toy mah-reh-ah'-doh. Tye'-neh oos-ted' ahl'-goh caun-trah el mah-reh'-oh?

We will be arriving in port in approximately 10 minutes' time

Llegaremos al puerto dentro de 10 minutos aproximadamente

Lyeh-gah-reh'-mos ahl pwer'-toh den'-troh deh dyeth' me-noo'-tohs ah-prauc-se-mah'-dah-men-teh

MEANS OF TRANSPORT IN TOWN

Bus	Autobús	*Ow-tau-boos'*
Underground	Metro	*Meh'-troh*
Taxi	Taxi	*Tac'-se*
Tram	Tranvía	*Tran-bee'-ah*
Ticket	Billete	*Be-lyeh'-teh*
Season ticket	Bono	*Bau'-noh*
Way in/Entrance	Entrada	*En-trah'-dah*
Way out/Exit	Salida	*Sah-lee'-dah*

By bus

Bus station ....

I want to go to ...
Quiero ir a ...
Kye'-roh eer ah ...

Two tickets, please
Dos billetes, por favor
Daus be-lyeh'-tehs, paur fah-baur'

How often do the buses run to ...?
¿Cada cuánto tiempo salen los autobuses para ...?
*Cah'-dah kwan'-toh tyem'-poh sah'-len lohs ow-tau-boo'-sehs
pah'-rah ...?*

How much does a single ticket cost?
¿Cuánto cuesta un billete de ida?
Kwan'-toh kwes'-tah oon be-lyeh'-teh deh ee'-dah?

Can I buy a ticket on the bus?
¿Puedo comprar el billete en el autobús?
Pweh'-doh caum-prar' el be-lyeh'-teh en el ow-tau-boos'?

Where must I get off for ...?
¿Dónde tengo que bajarme para ir a ...?
Daun'-deh ten'-goh keh bah-har'-meh pah'-rah eer ah ...?

Could I put this in the boot, please?
¿Podría poner esto en el maletero, por favor?
Pau-dree'-ah pau-ner' es'-toh en el mah-leh-teh'-roh, paur fah-baur'?

Is this seat vacant/taken?
¿Está libre/ocupado este asiento?
Es-tah' lee'-breh/au-coo-pah'-doh es'-teh ah-syen'-toh?

Could I see your ticket, please?
Billetes, por favor
Be-lyeh'-tehs, paur fah-baur'

I've lost my ticket
No encuentro mi billete
Noh en-kwehn'-troh mee be-lyeh'-teh

City buses ....

Bus stop
Parada de autobús
Pah-rah'-dah deh ow-tau-boos'

Request stop
Parada solicitada
Pah-rah'-dah sau-le-the-tah'-dah

Bell
Timbre
Teem'-breh

Exact fare
Importe exacto
Im-paur'-teh eh-xac'-toh

Do you know if the number ... bus goes past ...?
¿Sabe si el autobús número ... pasa por ...?
Sah'-beh see el ow-tau-boos' noo'-meh-roh... pah'-sah paur ...?

Which bus goes direct to ...?
¿Qué autobús va directo a ...?
Keh' ow-tau-boos' bah de-rec'-toh ah ...?

What's this stop?
¿Qué parada es esta?
Keh' pah-rah'-dah es es'-tah?

What's the next stop?
¿Cuál es la próxima parada?
Kwal' es lah prauc'-se-mah pah-rah'-dah?

This is my stop. I'm getting off here
Esta es mi parada. Me bajo aquí
Es'-tah es mee pah-rah'-dah. Meh bah'-hoh ah-kee'

UNDERGROUND

Underground/tube station
Estación de metro
Es-tah-thyon' deh meh'-troh

Entrance
Boca de metro
Bau'-cah deh meh'-troh

Escalator
Escaleras mecánicas
Es-cah-leh'-ras meh-cah'-ne-cas

Change lines
Transbordo
Trans-baur'-doh

One-month travelcard
Bono mensual
Bau'-noh men-swal'

Underground map
Plano del metro
Plah'-noh dehl meh'-troh

Platform	Andén/Vía	*An-den'/Bee'-ah*
Line	Línea	*Lee'-neh-ah*
Zone	Zona	*Thau'-nah*
Lift	Ascensor	*As-then-saur'*

Could you tell me where the nearest tube station is?
¿Podría decirme dónde está la estación de metro más próxima?
*Pau-dree'-ah deh-theer'-meh daun'-deh es-tah' lah es-tah-thyon' deh
meh'-troh mas prauc'-se-mah?*

Which line do I need for ...?
¿Qué línea debo tomar para ir a ...?
Keh' lee'-neh-ah deh'-boh tau-mar' pah'-rah eer ah ...?

Is this the right direction to go to ...?
¿Esta es la dirección para ...?
Es'-tah es lah de-rec-thyon' pah'-rah ...?

Mind the gap
Tengan cuidado al salir para no introducir el pie entre coche y andén
*Ten'-gan kwi-dah'-doh ahl sah-leer' pah'-rah noh in-trau-doo-theer' el
pye' en'-treh cau'-cheh ee an-den'*

TRAVELLING BY TAXI

Taxi rank
Parada de taxi
Pah-rah'-dah deh tac'-se

Receipt
Recibo/factura
Reh-thee'-boh/fac-too'-rah

For hire	Libre	*Lee'-breh*
Taximeter	Taxímetro	*Tac-see'-meh-troh*
Fare	Tarifa	*Tah-ree'-fah*

Where can I get a taxi?
¿Dónde puedo encontrar un taxi?
Daun'-deh pweh'-doh en-caun-trar' oon tac'-se?

Where would you like to go?
¿Adónde quiere ir?
Ah-daun'-deh kye'-reh eer?

Can you take me to ... street?
A la calle ..., por favor
Ah lah cah'-lyeh ..., paur fah-baur'

Do you know where ... is?
¿Sabe usted dónde está ...?
Sah'-beh oos-ted' daun'-deh es-tah' ...?

How much will it cost, more or less?
¿Cuánto me costará, más o menos?
Kwan'-toh meh caus-tah-rah', mas oh meh'-nohs?

Do you mind if I open/I close the window?
¿Le importa si abro/cierro la ventanilla?
Leh im-paur'-tah see ah'-broh/thyer'-roh lah ben-tah-nee'-lyah?

Stop here, please
Pare aquí, por favor
Pah'-reh ah-kee', paur fah-baur'

Could you wait for me here?
¿Puede esperarme un momento?
Pweh'-deh es-peh-rar'-meh oon mau-men'-toh?

Here you are
Ya hemos llegado
Yah eh'-mohs lyeh-gah'-doh

How much is it?/How much do I owe you?
¿Cuánto es?/¿Qué le debo?
Kwan'-toh es?/Keh' leh deh'-boh?

How much is the luggage supplement?
¿Cuál es el suplemento por equipaje?
Kwal' es el soo-pleh-men'-toh paur eh-ke-pah'-heh?

Have you got anything smaller?
¿No tiene un billete más pequeño?
Noh tye'-neh oon be-lyeh'-teh mas peh-keh'-nyoh?

That's fine, keep the change
Está bien, quédese con la vuelta
Es-tah' byen, keh'-deh-seh caun lah bwel'-tah

HOTELS

Hotel	Hotel	*Au-tehl'*
Guesthouse	Pensión, hostal	*Pen-syon', aus-tahl'*
Hostel	Albergue	*Al-ber'-gheh*
Accommodation	Alojamiento	*Ah-lau-hah-myen'-toh*
Stay	Estancia	*Es-tan'-thya*
Front desk	Recepción	*Reh-cep-thyon'*
Lobby	Vestíbulo	*Bes-tee'-boo-loh*
Receptionist	Recepcionista	*Reh-thep-thyo-nes'-ta*
Manager	Gerente	*Heh-ren'-teh*
Doorman	Portero	*Paur-teh'-roh*
Bellboy	Botones	*Bau-tau'-nes*
Chambermaid	Camarera	*Cah-mah-reh'-rah*
Guest	Huésped	*Wes'-ped*
Key	Llave	*Lyah'-beh*
Key card	Llave magnética	*Lyah'-beh mag-neh'-te-cah*
Safe	Caja fuerte	*Cah'-hah fwer'-teh*
Tip	Propina	*Prau-pee'-nah*
Lift	Ascensor	*As-then-saur'*
Floor	Piso (planta)	*Pee'-soh (plan'-tah)*

Ground flour
Planta baja
Plan'-tah bah'-hah

Dining room
Comedor
Cau-meh-daur'

Bathroom
Cuarto de baño
Kwar'-toh deh bah'-nyoh

Extra bed
Cama supletoria
Cah'-mah soo-pleh-tau'-rya

Low/high season
Temporada baja/alta
Tem-pau-rah'-dah bah'-hah/al'-tah

Single/double/twin-bedded room
Habitación individual/doble/con dos camas
Ah-be-tah-thyon' in-de-be-dwal'/dau'-bleh/caun daus cah'-mahs

Breakfast/half board/full board
Desayuno/media pensión/pensión completa
Deh-sah-yoo'-noh/meh'-dya pen-syon'/pen-syon' caum-pleh'-tah

MAKING A RESERVATION

Have you got any rooms?
¿Tienen habitaciones libres?
Tye'-nen ah-be-tah-thyo'-nehs lee'-brehs?

I'm sorry, we are full
Lo siento, está completo
Loh syen'-toh, es-tah' caum-pleh'-toh

We don't have any double/single room left
No nos queda ninguna habitación doble/individual
*Noh naus keh'-dah nin-goo'-nah ah-be-tah-thyon' dau'-bleh/
in-de-be-dwal'*

I'd like a room with …
Desearía una habitación con …
Deh-seh-ah-ree'-ah oo'-nah ah-be-tah-thyon' caun …

an en-suite bathroom
baño incluido
bah'-nyoh in-clwi'-doh

a sea view
vistas al mar
bees'-tahs ahl mar

Is breakfast included?

¿Incluido el desayuno?

In-clwi'-doh el deh-sah-yoo'-noh?

What's the price per night?

¿Cuál es el precio por noche?

Kwal' es el preh'-thyo paur nau'-cheh?

It's ... euros, including VAT

Son ... euros, IVA incluido

Saun ... eh'-oo-rohs, ee'-bah in-clwi'-doh

Does the room have air conditioning/television?

¿Tiene aire acondicionado/televisión?

Tye'-neh ah'-e-reh ah-caun-de-thyo-nah'-doh/teh-leh-be-syon'?

Is there a swimming pool/gym/sauna?

¿Hay piscina/gimnasio/sauna?

Ah'-y pes-thee'-nah/him-nah'-syo/sah'-oo-nah?

CHECKING IN

I've booked a room for ...

Tengo reservada una habitación a nombre de ...

Ten'-goh reh-ser-bah'-dah oo'-nah ah-be-tah-thyon' ah naum'-breh deh ...

Your room is number ... on the third floor, at the end of the corridor

Su habitación es la número ... en la tercera planta, al fondo del pasillo

Soo ah-be-tah-thyon' es lah noo'-meh-roh ... en lah ter-theh'-rah plan'-tah, ahl faun'-doh dehl pah-see'-lyoh

May I see the room?

¿Puedo ver la habitación?

Pweh'-doh ber lah ah-be-tah-thyon'?

It's all right. I'll take it

Está bien. Me quedo con ella

Es-tah' byen. Meh keh'-doh caun eh'-lyah

It's too small. Have you got another room bigger?

Es demasiado pequeña. ¿No tienen otra más amplia?

Es deh-mah-sya'-doh peh-keh'-nyah. Noh tye'-nen au'-trah mas ahm'-plya?

How long will you be staying?

¿Cuánto tiempo piensa quedarse?

Kwan'-toh tyem'-poh pyen'-sah keh-dar'-seh?

About five days

Unos cinco días

Oo'-nohs thin'-coh dee'-ahs

Can I see your passport, please?

¿Me permite su pasaporte?

Meh per-mee'-teh soo pah-sah-paur'-teh?

Sign here, please

Firme aquí, por favor

Feer'-meh ah-kee', paur fah-baur'

Send up my luggage, please

Súbanme el equipaje, por favor

Soo'-ban-meh el eh-ke-pah'-heh, paur fah-baur'

At what time is breakfast served?

¿A qué hora se sirve el desayuno?

Ah keh' au'-rah seh seer'-beh el deh-sah-yoo'-noh?

Please, wake me at seven

Haga el favor de despertarme a las siete

Ah'-gah el fah-baur' deh des-per-tar'-meh ah lahs sye'-teh

Claim	Queja	*Keh'-hah*
Bed	Cama	*Cah'-mah*
Mattress	Colchón	*Caul-chaun'*
Pillow	Almohada	*Al-moh-ah'-dah*
Blanket	Manta	*Man'-tah*
Duvet	Edredón	*Eh-dreh-daun'*
Sheets	Sábanas	*Sah'-bah-nas*
Tap	Grifo	*Gree'-foh*
Switch	Interruptor	*In-ter-roop-taur'*
Light bulb	Bombilla	*Baum-bee'-lyah*
Heating	Calefacción	*Cah-leh-fac-thyon'*
Air conditioning	Aire acondicionado	*Ah'-e-reh ah-caun-de-thyo-nah'-doh*
Ashtray	Cenicero	*Theh-ne-theh'-roh*
Wash basin	Lavabo	*Lah-bah'-boh*
Towel	Toalla	*Tau-ah'-lyah*
Soap	Jabón	*Hah-baun'*
Glass	Vaso	*Bah'-soh*

Bath towel
Toalla de baño
Tau-ah'-lyah deh bah'-nyoh

Toiletries
Artículos de tocador
Ar-tee'-coo-lohs deh toh-cah-daur'

Toothbrush
Cepillo de dientes
Theh-pee'-lyoh deh dyen'-tehs

Toothpaste
Pasta de dientes
Pas'-tah deh dyen'-tehs

Hairdryer
Secador
Seh-cah-daur'

Toilet paper
Papel higiénico
Pah-pehl ee-hye'-ne-coh

Do not disturb
No molestar
Noh mau-les-tar'

For the laundry
Para lavar
Pah'-rah lah-bar'

My key, please. Number ...
Mi llave, por favor. Número ...
Mee lyah'-beh, paur fah-baur'. Noo'-meh-roh ...

Serve my breakfast in my room
Súbanme el desayuno a la habitación
Soo'-ban-meh el deh-sah-yoo'-noh ah lah ah-be-tah-thyon'

Have you got a street map?
¿Tienen un plano de la ciudad?
Tye'-nen oon plah'-noh deh lah thew-dad'?

I can't open the door
No puedo abrir la puerta
Noh pweh'-doh ah-breer' lah pwer'-tah

The heating does not work
La calefacción no funciona
Lah cah-leh-fac-thyon' noh foon-thyo'-nah

There is no hot water
No hay agua caliente
Noh ah'-y ah'-gwa cah-lyen'-teh

Do you have another blanket, please?
Necesitaría una manta más
Neh-theh-se-tah-ree'-ah oo'-nah man'-tah mas

I want a guide who speaks English
Quiero un guía que hable inglés
Kye'-roh oon ghee'-ah keh ah'-bleh in-gles'

The switch in the bathroom does not work properly
El interruptor del cuarto de baño no funciona bien
El in-ter-roop-taur' dehl kwar'-toh deh bah'-nyoh noh foon-thyo'-nah byen

I want to hire a car
Quiero alquilar un coche
Kye'-roh al-ke-lar' oon cau'-cheh

HAVING BREAKFAST

Coffee	Café	*Cah-feh'*
Tea	Té	*Teh*
Milk	Leche	*Leh'-cheh*
Chocolate	Chocolate	*Choh-cau-lah'-teh*

Decaffeinated coffee	**Skim milk**
Descafeinado	Leche desnatada
Des-cah-fey-nah'-doh	*Leh'-cheh des-nah-tah'-dah*

Bread	Pan	*Pan*
Whole-grain bread	Pan integral	*Pan in-teh-grahl'*
Butter	Mantequilla	*Man-teh-kee'-lyah*
Yoghurt	Yogur	*Yoh-goor'*
Egg	Huevo	*Weh'-boh*
Toast	Tostada	*Taus tah'-dah*
Honey	Miel	*Myel'*

| **Corn flakes** | Cereales | *The-reh-ah'-lehs* |
| **Jam** | Mermelada | *Mer-meh-lah'-dah* |

Marmalade
Mermelada de naranja
Mer-meh-lah'-dah deh nah-ran'-hah

Orange juice
Zumo de naranja
Thoo'-moh deh nah-ran'-hah

Ham and eggs
Huevos con jamón
Weh'-bohs caun hah-maun'

Fried eggs
Huevos fritos
Weh'-bohs free'-tohs

May I have something to eat now?
¿Podría tomar algo a esta hora?
Pau-dree'-ah tau-mar' ahl'-goh ah es'-tah au'-rah?

The dining room is closed
El comedor está cerrado
El cau-meh-daur' es-tah' ther-rah'-doh

Put it on my bill. Room number ...
Cárguelo en mi cuenta. Habitación número ...
Car'-gheh-loh en mee kwehn'-tah. Ah-be-tah-thyon' noo'-meh-roh...

CHECKING OUT

We are leaving on ...
Nos vamos el ...
Naus bah'-mohs el ...

Could you make out my bill?

¿Puede prepararme la cuenta?

Pweh'-deh preh-pah-rar'-meh lah kwehn'-tah?

Have you used the minibar?

¿Ha utilizado el minibar?

Ah oo-te-le-thah'-doh el minibar'?

I think there is a mistake. Please check it

Creo que se ha equivocado. Repásela, por favor

Creh'-oh keh seh ah eh-ke-bau-cah'-doh. Reh-pah'-seh-lah, paur fah-baur'

I'll pay in cash/by credit card/by cheque

Voy a pagar en efectivo/con tarjeta de crédito/con un cheque

Boy ah pah-gar' en eh-fec-tee'-boh/caun tar-heh'-tah deh creh'-de-toh/caun oon cheh'-keh

Could I leave my luggage here until midday?

¿Puedo dejar mi equipaje aquí hasta mediodía?

Pweh'-doh deh-har' mee eh-ke-pah'-heh ah-kee' as'-tah meh-dyo-dee'-ah?

Could you please call me a taxi?

¿Podría llamar a un taxi, por favor?

Pau-dree'-ah lyah-mar'ah oon tac'-se, paur fah-baur'?

Have a good journey!

¡Buen viaje!

Bwen bya'-heh!

Thank you for everything!

¡Gracias por todo!

Grah'-thyas paur tau'-doh!

EATING AND DRINKING

Bar	Bar	*Bar*
Restaurant	Restaurante	*Res-tow-ran'-teh*

Fast food
Comida rápida
Cau-mee'-dah rah'-pe-dah

Takeaway
Comida para llevar
Cau-mee'-dah pah'-rah lyeh-bar'

Self-service
Autoservicio
Ow-tau-ser-bee'-thyo

Bar snacks
Tapas
Tah'-pahs

Set menú
Menú del día
Meh-noo' dehl dee'-ah

À la carte
A la carta
Ah lah car'-tah

Starter
Entrada
En-trah'-dah

Aperitif
Aperitivo
Ah-peh-re-tee'-boh

Main course
Plato principal
Plah'-toh prin-the-pahl'

Lunch
Almuerzo
Al-mwer'-thoh

Dinner
Cena
Theh'-nah

Dessert
Postre
Paus'-treh

"TAPAS"

Croquettes
Croquetas
Crau-keh'-tahs

Small brochettes
Pinchitos
Pin-chee'-tohs

Stuffed eggs
Huevos rellenos
Weh'-bohs reh-lyeh'-nohs

Tripe
Callos
Cah'-lyohs

Meatballs
Albóndigas
Al-baun'-de-gahs

Potato omelette
Tortilla de patatas
Taur-tee'-lyah deh pah-tah'-tahs

AT A RESTAURANT

Table	Mesa	*Meh'-sah*
Chair	Silla	*See'-lyah*
Tablecloth	Mantel	*Man-tehl'*
Napkin	Servilleta	*Ser-be-lyeh'-tah*
Dish	Plato	*Plah'-toh*
Spoon	Cuchara	*Coo-chah'-rah*
Fork	Tenedor	*Teh-neh-daur'*
Knife	Cuchillo	*Coo-chee'-lyoh*
Teaspoon	Cucharilla	*Coo-chah-ree'-lyah*
Glass	Vaso	*Bah'-soh*
(Wine) glass	Copa	*Cau'-pah*
Cup	Taza	*Tah'-thah*

Waiter	Camarero	*Cah-mah-reh'-roh*
Head waiter	Maitre	*Mehtr*
Tip	Propina	*Prau-pee'-nah*
Tip included	Servicio incluido	*Ser-bee'-thyo in-clwi'-doh*

Can you suggest a restaurant for local cuisine?
¿Puede recomendarme un restaurante típico?
Pweh'-deh reh-cau-men-dar'-meh oon res-tow-ran'-teh tee'-pe-coh?

Is there a bar near here?
¿Hay un bar cerca de aquí?
Ah'-y oon bar ther'-cah deh ah-kee'?

I'd like to book a table for ... people for ...
Quisiera reservar una mesa para ... personas para las ...
Ke-sye'-rah reh-ser-bar' oo'-nah meh'-sah pah'-rah ... per-sau'-nahs pah'-rah lahs ...

A table for two, please
Una mesa para dos, por favor
Oo'-nah meh'-sah pah'-rah daus, paur fah-baur'

Where can we sit?
¿Dónde podemos sentarnos?
Daun'-deh pau-deh'-mohs sen-tar'-nohs?

Is this table reserved?
¿Está reservada esta mesa?
Es-tah' reh-ser-bah'-dah es'-tah meh'-sah?

Can we have ...
¿Podemos tener ...
Pau-deh'-mohs teh-ner' ...

> **a table near the window?**
> una mesa cerca de la ventana?
> *oo'-nah meh'-sah ther'-cah deh lah ben-tah'-nah?*

a quiet table?

una mesa tranquila?

oo'-nah meh'-sah tran-kee'-lah?

a table away from the door?

una mesa lejos de la puerta?

oo'-nah meh'-sah leh'-hohs deh lah pwer'-tah?

You will have to wait in the bar

Tienen que esperar en la barra

Tye'-nen keh es-peh-rar' en lah bar'-rah

I'm waiting for some friends

Estoy esperando a unos amigos

Es-toy es-peh-ran'-doh ah oo'-nos ah-mee'-gohs

Can you bring me the menu?

¿Puede traerme la carta?

Pweh'-deh trah-er'-meh lah car'-tah?

What would you like?

¿Qué le sirvo?

Keh' leh seer'-boh?

I'd like a/an ...

Quiero un/una ...

Kye'-roh oon/oo'-nah ...

What would you like to drink?

¿Para beber?

Pah'-rah beh-ber?

Can you bring me an aperitif?

¿Puede traerme un aperitivo?

Pweh'-deh trah-er'-meh oon ah-peh-re-tee'-boh?

We haven't decided yet

No hemos elegido todavía

Noh eh'-mohs eh-leh-he'-doh

Have you got any hot dishes?

¿Tienen platos calientes?

Tye'-nen plah'-tohs cah-lyen'-tes?

What kind of ... have you got?

¿Qué tipo de ... tienen?

Keh' tee'-poh deh ... tye'-nen?

Could you suggest something special?

¿Puede recomendarme algo especial?

Pweh'-deh reh-cau-men-dar'-meh ahl'-goh es-peh-thyal'?

What is the local speciality?

¿Cuál es la especialidad de la casa?

Kwal' es lah es-peh-thya-le-dad' deh lah cah'-sah?

Have you got a wine list?

¿Tienen una carta de vinos?

Tye'-nen oo'-nah car'-tah deh bee'-nohs?

Which wine do you recommend?

¿Qué vino me recomienda?

Keh' bee'-noh meh reh-cau-myen'-dah?

What are the ingredients of this dish?

¿Cuáles son los ingredientes de este plato?

Kwa'-lehs saun lohs in-greh-dyen'-tehs deh es'-teh plah'-toh?

For my starter, bring me ...

De primero, tráigame ...

Deh pre-meh'-roh, trah'-e-gah-meh ...

For my main course, ...	**The same for me**
De segundo, ...	Lo mismo para mí
Deh seh-goon'-doh, ...	*Loh mees'-moh pah'-rah mee*

We did not asked for this

No hemos pedido esto

Noh eh'-mohs peh-de'-doh

Enough, thanks	**Enjoy your meal!**
Está bien, gracias	¡Buen provecho!
Es-tah' byen, grah'-thyas	*Bwen' prau-beh'-choh!*

Could I have ...
¿Puede traerme ...
Pweh'-deh trah-er'-meh ...

> **another bottle of wine**
> otra botella de vino
> *au'-trah boh-teh'-lyah deh bee'-noh*

> **some more bread**
> más pan
> *mas pan*

> **salt and pepper**
> sal y pimienta
> *sahl ee pe-myen'-tah*

This soup is cold. Could you heat it for me?
Esta sopa está fría. ¿Puede calentármela?
Es'-tah sau'-pah es-tah' free'-ah. Pweh'-deh cah-len-tar'-meh-lah?

This meat is underdone. Could you cook it a little more?
Esta carne está poco hecha. ¿Pueden pasarla un poco más?
Es'-tah car'-neh es-tah' pau'-coh eh'-chah. Pweh'-den pah-sar'-lah oon pau'-coh mas?

What is there for dessert?
¿Qué tienen de postre?
Keh' tye'-nen deh paus'-treh?

Will you have a coffee?
¿Tomarán café?
Tau-mah-ran' cah-feh'?

Have you finished?
¿Han terminado?
An ter-me-nah'-doh

The bill, please
La cuenta, por favor
Lah kwehn'-tah, paur fah-baur'

Do you accept credit cards?
¿Puedo pagar con tarjeta?
Pweh'-doh pah-gar' caun tar-heh'-tah?

I need the receipt
Necesito la factura
Neh-theh-see'-toh lah fac-too'-rah

Keep the change
Quédese con la vuelta
Keh'-deh-seh caun lah bwel'-tah

Have you got a lighter/light, please?
Por favor, ¿me da fuego?
Paur fah-baur', meh dah fweh'-goh?

Where is the toilet?
¿Dónde están los servicios?
Daun'-deh es-tan' lohs ser-bee'-thyos?

MEALS AND DRINKS

COOKING TERMS

Fried	Frito	*Free'-toh*
Boiled	Hervido	*Er-bee'-doh*
Roast(ed)	Asado	*Ah-sah'-doh*
Grilled	A la plancha	*A lah plan'-chah*
Toasted	Tostado	*Taus-tah'-doh*
Baked	Al horno	*Ahl aur'-noh*
Filled	Relleno	*Reh-lyeh'-noh*
Hot/spicy	Picante	*Pe-can'-teh*
Raw	Crudo	*Croo'-doh*
Sour	Agrio	*Ah'-gryo*
Smoked	Ahumado	*Ow-mah'-doh*
Salty	Salado	*Sah-ah'-doh*
Unsalted	Soso	*Sau'-soh*
Bitter	Amargo	*Ah-mar'-goh*
Sweet	Dulce	*Dool'-theh*
Sweet and sour	Agridulce	*Ah-gre-dool'-theh*
Rare (underdone)	Poco hecho	*Pau'-coh eh'-choh*
Medium	En su punto	*En soo poon'-toh*
Well done	Muy hecho	*Moo'-y eh'-choh*

SEASONING

Salt	Sal	*Sahl*
Pepper	Pimienta	*Pe-myen'-tah*
Spice	Especia	*Es-peh'-thya*
Oil	Aceite	*Ah-they'-teh*
Vinegar	Vinagre	*Be-nah'-greh*
Sauce	Salsa	*Sahl'-sah*
Mustard	Mostaza	*Maus-tah'-thah*
Mayonnaise	Mayonesa	*Mah-yoh-neh'-sah*
Paprika	Pimentón	*Pe-men-taun'*

HORS D'OEUVRES

Butter	Mantequilla	*Man-teh-kee'-lyah*
Bread	Pan	*Pan*
Olives	Aceitunas	*Ah-they-too'-nahs*
Cheese	Queso	*Keh'-soh*
Ham	Jamón	*Hah-maun'*
Cold meats/sausages	Embutidos	*Em-boo-tee'-dohs*

EGGS

Fried	Frito	*Free'-toh*
Soft-boiled	Pasado por agua	*Pah-sah'-doh paur ah'-gwa*
Hard-boiled	Duro	*Doo'-roh*
Scrambled	Revuelto	*Reh-bwehl'-toh*
Omelet	Tortilla	*Taur-tee'-lyah*

MEAT

Veal	Ternera	*Ter-neh'-rah*
Pork	Cerdo	*Ther'-doh*
Lamb	Cordero	*Caur-deh'-roh*

Beef	Buey	*Bweh'-y*
Chicken	Pollo	*Pau'-lyoh*
Duck	Pato	*Pah'-toh*
Turkey	Pavo	*Pah'-boh*
Rabbit	Conejo	*Cau-neh'-hoh*
Liver	Hígado	*Ee'-gah-doh*
Kidneys	Riñones	*Re-nyau'-nehs*
Loin	Lomo	*Lau'-moh*
Mince	Carne picada	*Car'-neh pe-cah'-dah*
Chop	Chuleta	*Choo-leh'-tah*
Rib	Costilla	*Caus-tee'-lyah*
Steak	Filete	*Fe-leh'-teh*
Sirloin	Solomillo	*Sau-lau-mee'-lyoh*
Roast beef	Rosbif	*Rohs'-beef*

FISH AND SEAFOOD

Sardine	Sardina	*Sar-dee'-nah*
Anchovy	Anchoa	*An-choh'-ah*
Tuna	Atún	*Ah-toon'*
Sole	Lenguado	*Len-gwa'-doh*
Hake	Merluza	*Mer-loo'-thah*
Cod	Bacalao	*Bah-cah-lah'-oh*
Salmon	Salmón	*Sal-maun'*
Red mullet	Salmonete	*Sal-mau-neh'-teh*
Swordfish	Pez espada	*Peth es-pah'-dah*
Sea bream	Besugo	*Beh-soo'-goh*
Trout	Trucha	*Troo'-chah*
Shrimp	Gamba	*Gahm'-bah*
Prawn	Langostino	*Lan-gaus-tee'-noh*
Lobster	Langosta	*Lan-gaus'-tah*
Mussel	Mejillón	*Meh-he-lyaun'*
Oyster	Ostra	*Aus'-trah*
Crab	Cangrejo	*Can-greh'-hoh*

VEGETABLES

Lettuce	Lechuga	*Leh-choo'-gah*
Tomato	Tomate	*Tau-mah'-teh*
Potato	Patata	*Pah-tah'-tah*
Cucumber	Pepino	*Peh-pee'-noh*
Onion	Cebolla	*Theh-bau'-lyah*
Garlic	Ajo	*Ah'-hoh*
Parsley	Perejil	*Peh-reh hool'*
(Green, red) pepper	Pimiento	*Pe-myen'-toh*
Carrot	Zanahoria	*Thah-nah-au'-rya*
Spinach	Espinaca	*Es-pe-nah'-cah*
Asparagus	Espárrago	*Es-par'-rah-goh*
Aubergine	Berenjena	*Beh-ren-heh'-nah*
Mushroom	Seta	*Seh'-tah*
Artichocke	Alcachofa	*Al-cah-chau'-fah*
Cabbage	Col	*Caul*
Cauliflower	Coliflor	*Cau-le-flaur'*
Green beans	Judías verdes	*Hoo-dee'-as ber'-des*
Celery	Apio	*Ah'-pyo*
Leek	Puerro	*Pwer'-roh*
Peas	Guisantes	*Ghee-san'-tehs*
Sweet corn	Maíz	*Mah-eeth'*
Beetroot	Remolacha	*Reh-moh-lah'-chah*
Pumpkin	Calabaza	*Cah-lah-bah'-thah*
Turnip	Nabo	*Nah'-boh*
Endive	Endivia	*En-dee'-bya*

FRUITS

Orange	Naranja	*Nah-ran'-hah*
Lemon	Limón	*Le-maun'*
Grapefruit	Pomelo	*Pau-meh'-loh*
Tangerine	Mandarina	*Man-dah-roo'-nah*
Apple	Manzana	*Man-thah'-nah*

Pear	Pera	*Peh'-rah*
Peach	Melocotón	*Meh-lau-cau- taun'*
Plum	Ciruela	*The-rweh'-lah*
Apricot	Albaricoque	*Al-bah-re-cau'-keh*
Cherry	Cereza	*Theh-reh'-thah*
Strawberry	Fresa	*Freh'-sah*
Raspberry	Frambuesa	*Fram-bweh'-sah*
Fig	Higo	*Ée-goh*
Grape	Uva	*Oo'-bah*
Banana	Plátano	*Plah'-tah-noh*
Melon	Melón	*Meh-laun'*
Watermelon	Sandía	*San-dee'-ah*
Pineapple	Piña	*Pee'-nyah*
Coconut	Coco	*Coh'-coh*
Almond	Almendra	*Ahl-men'-drah*

DRINKS

A glass of ...
Un vaso de ...
Oon bah'-soh deh ...

A cup of ...
Una taza de ...
Oo'-nah tah'-thah deh ...

Mineral water (sparkling/still)
Agua mineral (con/sin gas)
Ah'-gwa me-neh-rahl'
(caun/sin gahs)

Orange juice
Zumo de naranja
Thoo'-moh deh nah-ran'-hah

Lemonade	Gaseosa	*Gah-seh-au'-sah*
Soft drink	Refresco	*Reh-fres'-coh*
Beer	Cerveza	*Ther-beh'-thah*
Draft beer	Caña	*Cah'-nyah*
Tankard	Jarra	*Har'-rah*

Alcohol-free beer
Cerveza sin alcohol
Ther-beh'-thah sin al-cau-aul'

(White/Red/Rosé) wine
Vino (blanco/tinto/rosado)
Bee'-noh blan'-coh/tin'-toh/
rau-sah'-doh

Dry	Seco	*Seh'-coh*
Sweet	Dulce	*Dool'-theh*
Vintage	Cosecha	*Cau-seh'-chah*
Sherry	Jerez	*Heh-reth'*
Champagne	Champán	*Chahm-pan'*
Liqueur	Licor	*Le-caur'*
Rum	Ron	*Rohm*
Gin	Ginebra	*He-neh'-brah*
Brandy	Coñac	*Cau-nyac'*
Whisky	Whisky	*Goo-is'-kee*
On the rocks	Con hielo	*Caun ye'-loh*
Herbal tea	Infusión	*In-foo-syon'*

White coffee
Café con leche
Cah-feh' caun leh'-cheh

Black coffee
Café solo
Cah-feh' sau'-loh

Decaffeinated coffee
Descafeinado
Des-cah-fey-nah'-doh

Cold/hot milk
Leche fría/caliente
Leh'-cheh free'-ah/cah-lyen'-teh

Tea with lemon/milk
Té con limón/leche
Teh caun le-maun'/leh'-cheh

Hot chocolate
Chocolate caliente
Chau-cau-lah'-teh cah-lyen'-teh

TAPAS (BAR SNACKS)

Albóndigas con tomate *(Al-baun'-de-gahs caun toh-mah'-teh)*.
Meatballs with tomato sauce.

Berenjenas fritas con miel *(Beh-ren-heh'-nahs free'-thas caun myel')*. Deep-fried aubergine with honey.

Boquerones en vinagre *(Bau-keh-rau'-nehs en be-nah'-greh)*. White anchovies in vinegar.

Buñuelos de bacalao *(Boo-nyweh'-lohs deh bah-cah-lah'-oh)*. Salt cod fritters.

Callos con garbanzos *(Cah'-lyohs caun gar-ban'-thohs)*. Tripe stew with chickpeas.

Champiñones al ajillo *(Cham-pe-nyoh'-nehs ahl ah-he'-lyoh)*. Garlic mushrooms.

Croquetas de jamón *(Crau-keh'-tahs deh hah-maun')*. Serrano ham croquettes.

Ensaladilla rusa *(En-sah-lah-dee'-lyah roo'-sah)*. Russian salad.

Gambas al pil-pil *(Gam'-bahs ahl peel-peel')*. Chilli & garlic prawns.

Habas con jamón *(Ah'-bahs caun hah-maun')*. Broad beans and ham.

Huevos rellenos *(Weh'-bohs reh-lyeh'-nohs)*. Stuffed eggs.

Pulpo a la gallega *(Pool'-poh ah lah gah-lyeh'-gah)*. Galician style octopus.

Riñones al jerez *(Re-nyoh'-nehs ahl heh-reth')*. Kidneys in Sherry sauce.

Tortilla de patatas *(Taur-tee'-lyah deh pah-tah'-tahs)*. Potato omelette.

TYPICAL SPANISH FOOD

Besugo al horno *(Beh-soo'-goh ahl aur'-noh)*. Baked sea bream.

Caracoles en salsa *(Cah-rah-cau'-lehs en sahl'-sah)*. Snails in hot sauce.

Cocido madrileño *(Cau-thee'-doh mah-dre-leh'-nyoh)*. Stew combining chickpeas with vegetables (cabbage, celery, carrots, turnips and potatoes) and chicken, beef and pork.

Gazpacho *(Gath-pah'-choh)*. Cold tomato-cucumber soup.

Paella *(Pah-eh'-lyah)*. Rice, chicken and seafood casserole.

Potaje de legumbres *(Poh-tah'-heh deh leh-goom'-brehs)*. Vegetable stew.

Sopa de ajo *(Sau'-pah deh ah'-hoh)*. Garlic soup.

Sopa de mariscos *(Sau'-pah deh mah-rees'-cohs)*. Seafood soup.

DESSERTS

Pie	Pastel	*Pas-tehl'*
Cake	Tarta	*Tar'-tah*
Ice cream	Helado	*Eh-lah'-doh*
Cream	Nata	*Nah'-tah*
Custard	Natillas	*Nah-tee'-lyahs*
Caramel custard	Flan	*Flahn*
Cheese	Queso	*Keh'-soh*

Fruit salad	**Rice pudding**
Macedonia de frutas	Arroz con leche
Mah-theh-dau'-nya deh froo'-tas	*Ar-rauth' caun leh'-cheh*

Typical Spanish desserts ....

Crema catalana *(Creh'-mah cah-tah-lah'-nah)*. A custard-like base with a layer of burnt sugar.

Cuajada *(Kwa-hah'-dah)*. Curds.

Leche frita *(Leh'-cheh free'-tah)*. A sweet batter of milk and flour which is fried in breadcrumbs.

Tarta de manzana *(Tar'-tah deh man-thah'-nah)*. Apple pie.

Tocino de cielo *(Tau-thee'-noh deh thye'-loh)*. Dessert made with eggs yolks mixed with sugar.

Torrijas *(Taur-ree'-hahs)*. Slices of bread soaked in cinnamon-flavoured milk, fried and dipped in honey or sugar.

SHOPPING

English	Spanish	Pronunciation
Antique shop	Antigüedades	*An-te-gweh-dah'-dehs*
Baker's	Panadería	*Pah-nah-deh-ree'-ah*
Bookshop	Librería	*Le-breh-ree'-ah*
Butcher's	Carnicería	*Car-ne-theh-ree'-ah*
Cake shop/patisserie	Pasteleria	*Pas-teh-leh-ree'-ah*
Chemist's	Farmacia	*Far-mah'-thya*
Ironmonger's	Ferretería	*Fer-reh-teh-ree'-ah*
Delicatessen	Charcutería	*Char-coo-teh-ree'-ah*
Dry cleaning	Tintorería	*Teen-tau-reh-ree'-ah*
Fish shop	Pescadería	*Pes-cah-deh-ree'-ah*
Florist's	Floristería	*Flau-res-teh-ree'-ah*
Greengrocer's	Frutería	*Froo-teh-ree'-ah*
Hairdresser's	Peluquería	*Peh-loo-keh-ree'-ah*
Handicraft	Artesanía	*Ar-teh-sah-nee'-ah*
Herbalist shop	Herboristería	*Er-bau-res-teh-ree'-ah*
Jeweller's	Joyería	*Hau-yeh-ree'-ah*
Laundry	Lavandería	*Lah-ban-deh-ree'-ah*
Market	Mercado	*Mer-cah'-doh*
Newsagent's	Quiosco	*Kyos'-coh*
Optician's	Óptica	*Aup'-te-cah*
Perfumery	Perfumería	*Per-foo-meh-ree'-ah*
Shoe shop	Zapatería	*Thah-pah-teh-ree'-ah*
Souvenir	Recuerdo	*Reh-kwer'-doh*
Stationer's	Papelería	*Pah-peh-leh-ree'-ah*
Supermarket	Supermercado	*Soo-per-mer-cah'-doh*
Ten-cent store	Todo a cien	*Tau'-doh ah thyen'*
Tobacconist's	Estanco	*Es-tan'-coh*

Department store
Grandes almacenes
Gran'-des al-mah-theh'-nehs

Grocer's
Tienda de comestibles
Tyen'-dah deh cau-mes-tee'-bles

Photography equipment store		Shopping centre	
Tienda de fotos		Centro comercial	
Tyen'-dah deh fau'-tohs		*Then'-troh cau-mer-thyal'*	

Opening hours	Horario comercial	*Au-rah'-ryo*
		cau-mer-thyal'
Open	Abierto	*Ah-byer'-toh*
Closed	Cerrado	*Ther-rah'-doh*
Entrance	Entrada	*En-trah'-dah*
Exit	Salida	*Sah-lee'-dah*
Pull	Tirar	*Te-rar'*
Push	Empujar	*Em-poo-har'*
Lift	Ascensor	*As-then-saur'*
Shelf	Estantería	*Es-tan-teh-ree'-ah*
Counter	Mostrador	*Maus-trah-daur'*
Stairs	Escaleras	*Es-cah-leh'-rahs*
Cashdesk	Caja	*Cah'-hah*
Bag	Bolsa	*Baul'-sah*
Aisle	Pasillo	*Pah-see'-lyoh*

Escalator
Escaleras mecánicas
Es-cah-leh'-ras meh-cah'-ne-cas

Fire exit
Salida de emergencia
Sah-lee'-dah deh eh-mer-hen'-thya

Shop window
Escaparate
Es-cah-pah-rah'-teh

Shop assistant
Dependiente/a
Deh-pen-dyen'-teh/tah

Store card
Tarjeta de compra
Tar-heh'-tah deh caum'-prah

Cheques not accepted
No se admiten cheques
Noh seh ad-mee'-ten cheh'-kehs

Delivery
Envío a domicilio
En-by'oh ah doh-me-thee'-lyo

Complaint book
Libro de reclamaciones
Lee'-broh deh
reh-clah-mah-thyo'-nehs

Will you pay cash or by credit card?
¿En efectivo o con tarjeta?
En eh-fec-tee'-boh au caun tar-heh'-tah?

At the supermarket

Trolley	Carrito	*Cah-rree'-toh*
Shopping basket	Cesta	*Thes'-tah*
Checkout	Caja	*Cah'-hah*
Special offer	Oferta	*Au-fer'-tah*
Bottle	Botella	*Bau-teh'-lyah*
Box	Caja	*Cah'-hah*
Packet	Paquete	*Pah-keh'-teh*
Pot	Tarro	*Tar'-roh*
Tin	Lata	*Lah'-tah*
Piece	Trozo	*Trau'-thoh*

Slice
Loncha/rodaja
Laun'-chah/rau-dah'-hah

Dozen/half dozen
Docena/media docena
Dau-theh'-nah/meh'-dya dau-theh'-nah

10 items or less
Caja rápida 10 artículos
Cah'-hah rah'-pe-dah dyeth' ar-tee'-coo-lohs

Best before end ...
Consumir preferentemente antes de ...
Caun-soo-meer' preh-feh-ren'-teh-men-teh an'-tes deh ...

Where is the nearest supermarket?
¿Hay un supermercado por aquí cerca?
Ah'-y oon soo-per-mer-cah'-doh paur ah-kee' ther'-cah?

Could you tell me where the ... is (are)?
¿Podría decirme dónde está(n) ...?
Pau-dree'-ah deh-theer'-meh daun'-deh es-tah'(n) ...?

frozen food section	**household goods**
congelados	artículos del hogar
caun-heh-lah'-dohs	*ar-tee'-coo-lohs dehl au-gar'*

dairy products	**bread counter**
lácteos	*el pan*
lac'-teh-ohs	*el pan*

Could I have another carrier bag, please?
¿Puede darme otra bolsa, por favor?
Pweh'-deh dar'-meh au'-trah baul'-sah, paur fah-baur'?

Book	Libro	*Lee'-broh*
Dictionary	Diccionario	*Dic-thyo-nah-ryo*
Novel	Novela	*Nau-beh'-lah*
Postcard	Postal	*Paus-tahl'*
Newspaper	Periódico	*Peh-ryo'-de-coh*
Magazine	Revista	*Reh-bees'-tah*
Ballpoint pen	Bolígrafo	*Bau-lee'-grah-foh*
Pen	Pluma	*Ploo'-mah*
Pencil	Lápiz	*Lah'-pith*
Marker pen	Rotulador	*Rau-too-lah-daur'*
Envelope	Sobre	*Sau'-breh*

Guide	Guía	*Ghee'-ah*
Map	Mapa	*Mah'-pah*
Street map	Plano	*Plah'-noh*

I'd like ...

Quería/quisiera ...

Keh-ree'-ah/ke-sye'-rah ...

I'm looking for a book by/on ... Can you help me?

Estoy buscando un libro de/sobre ... ¿Puede ayudarme?

Es-toy boos-can'-doh oon lee'-broh deh/sau'-breh ... Pweh'-deh ah-yoo-dar'-meh?

I'd like a book concerning the history and art of this city

Quisiera un libro sobre la historia y el arte de esta ciudad

Ke-sye'-rah oon lee'-broh sau'-breh lah is-tau'-rya ee el ar'-teh deh es'-tah thew-dad'

Is it translated into English?

¿Está traducido al inglés?

Es-tah' trah-doo-thee'-doh ahl in-gles'?

¿Dónde puedo comprar un mapa de carreteras?

Where can I buy a road map?

Daun'-deh pweh'-doh caum-prar' oon mah'-pah deh car-reh-teh'-ras?

Have you got English newspapers/magazines/books?

¿Tiene periódicos/revistas/libros ingleses?

Tye'-neh peh-ryo'-de-cohs/reh-bees'-tahs/lee'-brohs in-gleh'-sehs?

Duty chemist	Farmacia de guardia	*Far-mah'-thya deh gwar'-dya*
Prescription	Receta	*Reh-theh'-tah*
Painkiller	Analgésico	*Ah-nahl-heh'-se-coh*
Tablet	Pastilla	*Pas-tee'-lyah*
Pill	Píldora	*Peel'-dau-rah*
Syrup	Jarabe	*Hah-rah'-beh*
Cream	Pomada	*Pau-mah'-dah*
Suppository	Supositorio	*Soo-pau-se-tau'-ryo*
Drops	Gotas	*Gau'-tahs*
Laxative	Laxante	*Lac-san'-teh*
Sedative	Calmante	*Cal-man'-teh*
Injection	Inyección	*In-yec-thyon'*
Bandage	Venda	*Ben'-dah*
Sticking plasters	Tiritas	*Te-ree'-tahs*
Cotton wool	Algodón	*Al-gau-daun'*
Gauze	Gasa	*Gah'-sah*
Alcohol	Alcohol	*Al-cau-aul'*
Thermometer	Termómetro	*Ter-mau'-mch-troh*
Condoms	Preservativos	*Preh-ser-bah-tee'-bos*
Sanitary towels	Compresas	*Caum-preh'-sahs*
Napkins	Pañales	*Pah-nyah-lehs'*

Toothpaste
Pasta de dientes
Pas'-tah deh dyen'-tehs

Toothbrush
Cepillo de dientes
Theh-pee'-lyoh deh dyen'-tehs

Paper tissues
Pañuelos de papel
Pah-nyweh'-los deh pah-pehl'

Earplugs
Tapones para los oídos
Tah-pau'-nes pah'-rah lohs oy'-dos

Could you give me anything for ...?
¿Puede darme algo contra ...?
Pweh'-deh dar'-meh ahl'-goh caun'-trah ...?

fever	fiebre	*fye'-breh*
cold	resfriado	*res-frya'-doh*
cough	tos	*taus*
diarrhoea	diarrea	*de-ar-reh'-ah*
constipation	estreñimiento	*es-treh-nye-myen-toh*
sickness	mareo	*mah-reh'-oh*
insomnia	insomnio	*in-saum'-nyo*

headache
dolor de cabeza
dau-laur' deh cah-beh'-thah

toothache
dolor de muelas
dau-laur' deh mweh'-lahs

sunburn
quemadura del sol
keh-mah-doo'-rah dehl saul

insect bite
picadura de insecto
pe-cah-doo'-rah deh in-sec'-toh

Take one tablet with breakfast, lunch and dinner
Tómese un comprimido en el desayuno, almuerzo y cena
Tau'-meh-seh oon caum-pre-mee'-doh en el deh-sah-yoo'-noh, al-mwer'-thoh ee theh'-nah

This medicine is only available on prescription
No podemos venderle este medicamento sin receta
Noh pau-deh'-mohs ben-der'-leh es'-teh meh-de-cah-men'-toh sin reh-theh'-tah

At a department store

Sales	Rebajas	*Reh-bah'-hahs*
Clearance sale	Liquidación	*Le-ke-dah-thyon'*
Bargain	Oportunidades	*Au-paur-too-ne-dah'-dehs*
Fitting room	Probador	*Prau-bah-daur'*

Ground floor
Planta baja
Plan'-tah bah'-hah

First, second, ... floor
Primera, segunda, ... planta
Pre-meh'-rah, seh-goon'-dah... plan'-tah

Record/gift/lingerie/toy/sport ... department
Sección de discos/regalos/lencería/juguetes/deportes ...
Sec-thyon' deh dees'-cohs/reh-gah'-los/len-theh-ry'ah/hoo-gheh'-tes/ deh-paur'-tes ...

Mens's/women's/children's clothes
Ropa de caballero/señora/niños
Rau'-pah deh cah-bah-lyeh'-roh/seh-nyau'-rah/nee'-nyohs

Small/medium/large
Talla pequeña/mediana/grande
Tah'-lyah peh-keh'-nyah/meh-dya'-nah/gran'-deh

In which floor is the leather goods department?
¿En qué planta está la sección de artículos de piel?
En keh' plan'-tah es-tah' lah sec-thyon' deh ar-tee'-coo-lohs deh pyel'?

On the ground floor
En la planta baja
En lah plan'-tah bah'-hah

Excuse me, could you help me?
¿Puede atenderme, por favor?
Pweh'-deh ah-ten-der'-meh, paur fah-baur'?

I'd like to see some striped shirts
Quisiera ver algunas camisas de rayas
Ke-sye'-rah ber al-goo'-nahs cah-mee'-sahs deh rah'-yahs

I want it with short/long sleeves
La quiero de manga corta/larga
Lah kye'-roh deh man'-gah caur'-tah/lar'-gah

What material is it?
¿De qué es?
Deh keh' es?

Is this the only colour you've got?
¿Sólo lo tienen en este color?
Sau'-loh loh tye'-nen en es'-teh cau-laur'?

Have you got any other designs?
¿Tienen otros modelos?
Tye'-nen au'-trohs mau-deh'-lohs?

What size do you take?
¿Cuál es su talla?
Kwal' es soo tah'-lyah?

Do you want to try it on?
¿Desea probárselo?
Deh-seh'-ah prau-bar'-seh-loh?

Where is the fitting room?
¿Dónde está el probador?
Daun'-deh es-tah' el prau-bah-daur'?

Does it fit you?
¿Le queda bien?
Leh keh'-dah byen?

The collar is a little tight
El cuello me aprieta un poco
El kweh'-lyoh meh ah-prye'-tah oon pau'-coh

I'll try a larger size
Voy a probarme una talla mayor
Boy ah prau-bar'-meh oo'-nah tah'-lyah mah-yaur'

I'll take this one
Me quedo con éste/a
Meh keh'-doh caun es'-teh/-ah

I like this one
Me gusta éste/a
Meh goos'-tah es'-teh/-ah

Please, show me some natural silk ties
Por favor, enséñeme corbatas de seda natural
Paur fah-baur', en-seh'-nyeh-meh caur-bah'-tahs deh seh'-dah nah-too-rahl'

How much is that all together?
¿Cuánto es todo?
Kwan'-toh es tau'-doh?

Where is the cashdesk?
¿Dónde está la caja?
Daun'-deh es-tah' lah cah'-hah?

Will you pay cash or by credit card?
¿En efectivo o con tarjeta?
En eh-fec-tee'-boh au caun tar-heh'-tah?

Could you gift-wrap it for me?
¿Podría envolvérmelo para regalo?
Pau-dree'-ah en-baul-ber'-meh-loh pah'-rah reh-gah'-loh?

CLOTHES AND ACCESSORIES

Overcoat	Abrigo	*Ah-bree'-goh*
Raincoat	Impermeable	*Im-per-meh-ah'-bleh*
Trench coat	Gabardina	*Gah-bar-dee'-nah*
Bomber jacket	Cazadora	*Cah-thah-dau'-rah*
Trousers	Pantalones	*Pan-tah-lau'-nehs*
Shorts	Pantalones cortos	*Pan-tah-lau'-nehs caur'-tohs*

Jeans	Vaqueros	*Bah-keh'-rohs*
Pullover	Jersey	*Her-seh'-y*
Jacket	Chaqueta	*Chah-keh'-tah*
T-shirt	Camiseta	*Cah-me-seh'-tah*
Waistcoat	Chaleco	*Chah-leh'-coh*
Vest	Camiseta	*Cah-me-seh'-tah*
Underpants	Calzoncillos	*Cal-thaun-thee'-lyohs*
Socks	Calcetines	*Cal-theh-tee'-nes*
Tie	Corbata	*Caur-bah'-tah*
Shirt	Camisa	*Cah-mee'-sah*
Blouse	Blusa	*Bloo'-sah*
Skirt	Falda	*Fahl'-dah*
Cardigan	Rebeca	*Reh-beh'-cah*
Suit	Traje	*Trah'-heh*
Dress	Vestido	*Bes-tee'-doh*
Evening dress	Traje de noche	*Trah'-heh deh nau'-cheh*
Bra	Sujetador	*Soo-heh-tah-daur'*
Tights	Medias	*Meh'-dyas*
Knickers	Bragas	*Brah'-gahs*
Dressing gown	Bata	*Bah'-tah*
Pyjamas	Pijama	*Pe-hah'-mah*
Night gown	Camisón	*Cah-me-saun'*
Bathing costume	Bañador	*Bah-nyah-daur'*
Tracksuit	Chándal	*Chan'-dal*
Sweat shirt	Sudadera	*Soo-dah-deh'-rah*
Gloves	Guantes	*Gwan'-tehs*
Scarf	Bufanda	*Boo-fan'-dah*
Umbrella	Paraguas	*Pah-rah'-gwahs*
Handkerchief	Pañuelo	*Pah-nyweh'-loh*
Belt	Cinturón	*Thin-too-raun'*
Handbag	Bolso	*Baul'-soh*
Purse	Monedero	*Mau-neh-deh'-roh*
Hat	Sombrero	*Saum-breh'-roh*
Fan	Abanico	*Ah-bah-nee'-coh*

Ring	Anillo	*Ah-nee'-lyoh*
Earring	Pendiente	*Pen-dyen'-teh*
Bracelet	Pulsera	*Pool-seh'-rah*

Materials

Cotton	Algodón	*Al-gau-daun'*
Leather	Piel	*Pyel'*
Linen	Lino	*Loo' noh*
Wool	Lana	*Lah'-nah*
Velvet	Terciopelo	*Ter-thyo-peh'-loh*
Silk	Seda	*Seh'-dah*
Viscose	Viscosa	*Bes-cau'-sah*
Nylon	Nilón	*Ne-laun'*
Acrilic fibre	Acrílico	*Ah-cree'-le-coh*

Colours

White	Blanco	*Blan'-coh*
Black	Negro	*Neh'-groh*
Red	Rojo	*Rau'-hoh*
Blue	Azul	*Ah-thool'*
Yellow	Amarillo	*Ah-mah-ree'-lyoh*
Brown	Marrón	*Mar-raun'*
Green	Verde	*Ber'-deh*
Grey	Gris	*Grees*
Beige	Beige	*Beysh*
Purple	Morado	*Mau-rah'-doh*
Orange	Naranja	*Nah-ran'-hah*
Pink	Rosa	*Rau'-sah*
Light	Claro	*Clah'-roh*
Dark	Oscuro	*Aus-coo'-roh*

Striped	A rayas	*Ah rah'-yahs*
Checked	A cuadros	*Ah kwa'-dros*
Pattern	Estampado	*Es-tam-pah'-doh*
Plain	Liso	*Lee'-soh*

Shoes	Zapatos	*Thah-pah'-tohs*
Boots	Botas	*Bau'-tahs*
Ankle boots	Botines	*Bau-tee'-nehs*
Sandals	Sandalias	*San-dah'-lyas*
Flip-flops	Chanclas	*Chan'-clahs*
Moccasins	Mocasines	*Mau-cah-see'-nehs*
Slippers	Zapatillas	*Thah-pah-tee'-lyahs*
Trainers/Sneakers	Zapatillas de deporte	*Thah-pah-tee'-lyahs deh deh-paur'-teh*
Sole	Suela	*Sweh'-lah*
Heel	Tacón	*Tah-caun'*
Shoelace	Cordón	*Caur-daun'*
Leather	Piel	*Pyel'*
Suede	Ante	*An'-teh*
Rubber	Goma	*Gau'-mah*

I want a pair of high-heeled shoes
Deseo un par de zapatos de tacón alto
Deh-seh'-oh oon par deh thah-pah'-tohs deh tah-caun' ahl'-toh

What style would you like?
¿Cómo los quiere?
Cau'-moh lohs kye'-reh?

With shoelaces and good for the rain
Con cordones y que sean buenos para la lluvia
Caun caur-dau'-nehs ee keh seh'-an bweh'-nohs pah'-rah lah lyoo'-bya

What size, please?
¿Qué número calza?
Keh' noo'-meh-roh cahl'-thah?

Will you please show me the pair in the window
Haga el favor de enseñarme los del escaparate
Ah'-gah el fah-baur' deh en-seh-nyar'-meh lohs dehl
es-cah-pah-rah'-teh

They are a little tight
Me aprietan un poco
Meh ah-prye'-tan oon pau'-coh

They are too large
Me quedan demasiado grandes
Meh keh'-dan deh-mah-sya'-doh gran'-dehs

Try this size
Pruébese este otro número
Prweh'-beh-seh es'-teh au'-troh noo'-meh-roh

This one fits well
Estos me están bien
Es'-tohs meh es-tan' byen

How much are they?
¿Cuánto valen?
Kwan'-toh bah'-len?

Soap	Jabón	*Hah-baun'*
Shampoo	Champú	*Cham-poo'*
Deodorant	Desodorante	*Deh-sau-dau-ran'-teh*
Shower gel	Gel de baño	*Hehl deh bah'-nyoh*
Hair spray	Laca	*Lah'-cah*
Comb	Peine	*Pey-neh*
Hairbrush	Cepillo	*Theh-pee'-lyoh*
Cotton buds	Bastoncillos	*Bas-ton-thee'-lyohs*
Make up	Maquillaje	*Mah-ke-lyah'-heh*
Cologne water	Colonia	*Cau-lau'-nya*
Nail varnish	Esmalte	*Es-mahl'-teh*
Mascara	Rímel	*Ree'-mel*
Perfume	Perfume	*Per-foo'-meh*
Hair remover	Depilatorio	*Deh-pe-lah-tau'-ryo*
Scissors	Tijeras	*Te-heh'-rahs*

Sun tan cream
Bronceador
Braun-theh-ah-daur'

Lipstick
Barra de labios
Bar'-rah deh lah'-byos

Toothbrush
Cepillo de dientes
Theh-pee'-lyoh deh dyen'-tehs

Toothpaste
Pasta de dientes
Pas'-tah deh dyen'-tehs

Dental floss
Hilo dental
Ée-loh den-tahl'

Face lotion
Loción facial
Lau-thyon' fah-thyal'

Cleansing cream
Crema limpiadora
Creh'-mah lim-pya-dau'-rah

Nourishing cream
Crema nutritiva
Creh'-mah noo-tre-tee'-bah

Razor
Maquinilla de afeitar
Mah-ke-nee'-lyah deh ah-fey-tar'

Shaving foam
Espuma de afeitar
Es-poo'-mah deh ah-fey-tar'

Camera	Cámara	Cah'-mah-rah
Digital camera	Cámara digital	Cah'-mah-rah de-he-tahl'
Lens	Objetivo	Aub-heh-tee'-boh
View-finder	Visor	Be-saur'
Filter	Filtro	Feel'-troh
Diaphragm	Diafragma	Dya-frag'-mah
Trigger	Disparador	Dis-pah-rah-daur'
Telephoto lens	Teleobjetivo	Teh-leh-ob-heh-te'-boh
Screen	Pantalla	Pan-tah'-lyah
Colour	Color	Cau-laur'
Black and white	Blanco y negro	Blan'-coh ee neh'-groh
Slide	Diapositiva	Dya-pau-se-tee'-bah
Size	Tamaño	Tah-mah'-nyoh
Enlargement	Ampliación	Am-plya-thyon'
Print	Copia	Cau'-pya
Photo/Picture	Foto	Fau'-toh
Battery	Batería	Bah-teh-ree'-ah
Battery charger	Cargador	Car-gah-daur'
Gloss	Brillo	Bree'-lyoh
Matt	Mate	Mah'-teh

Can you enlarge these prints?
¿Puede ampliarme estas copias?
Pweh'-deh am-ple-ar'-meh es'-tahs cau'-pyas?

Do you take passport photos?
¿Hacen fotos de carné?
Ah'-then fau'-tohs deh car-neh'?

My camera won't work, can you see what is wrong with it?
Mi cámara no funciona, ¿puede usted ver qué le pasa?
Mee cah'-mah-rah noh foon-thyo'-nah, pweh'-deh oos-ted' ber keh' leh pah'-sah?

AT THE OPTICIAN'S

Glasses	Gafas	*Gah'-fahs*
Lens	Cristal	*Cris-tahl'*
Frame	Montura	*Maun-too'-rah*

Contact lenses
Lentes de contacto (lentillas)
Len'-tehs deh caun-tac'-toh
(len-tee'-lyahs)

Sun glasses
Gafas de sol
Gah'-fahs deh saul

I'd like to have an eye test, please
Necesito que me gradúe la vista, por favor
Neh-theh-se'-toh keh meh grah-doo'-eh lah bees'-tah, paur fah-baur'

Are you long-sighted or short-sighted?
¿Ve mal de cerca o de lejos?
Beh mahl deh ther'-cah oh deh leh'-hohs?

Can you read out the letters on the chart?
¿Puede leer las letras del panel?
Pweh'-deh leh-er' lahs leh'-trahs dehl pah-nehl'?

I need a pair of reading glasses
Necesito gafas para leer
Neh-theh-see'-toh gah'-fahs pah'-rah leh-er'

The frame/a lens on these glasses is broken
Se me ha roto la montura/un cristal de las gatas
Seh meh ah rau'-toh lah maun-too'-rah/oon cris-tahl'deh lahs gah'-fahs

Can you repair it?
¿Puede repararlo?
Pweh'-deh reh-pah-rar'-loh?

When will they be ready?
¿Cuándo estarán listas?
Kwan'-doh es-tah-ran' lees'-tahs?

I'm looking for some cleaning fluid for contact lenses
Necesito un líquido limpiador de lentillas
Neh-theh-see'-toh oon lee'-ke-doh lim-pya-daur' deh len-tee'-lyahs

AT THE FLORIST'S

Rose	Rosa	*Rau'-sah*
Carnation	Clavel	*Clah-behl'*
Daisy	Margarita	*Mar-gah-ree'-tah*
Orchid	Orquídea	*Aur-kee'-deh-ah*
Iris	Lirio	*Lee'-ryo*
White lily	Azucona	*Ah thoo thch' nah*
Violet	Violeta	*Byo-leh'-tah*

Pansy	Pensamiento	*Pen-sah-myen'-toh*
Dahlia	Dalia	*Dah'-lya*
Spikenard	Nardo	*Nar'-doh*
Gardenia	Gardenia	*Gar-deh'-nya*
Hyacinth	Jacinto	*Hah-thin'-toh*
Daffodil	Narciso	*Nar-thee'-soh*
Chrysanthemum	Crisantemo	*Cri-san-teh'-moh*
Tulip	Tulipán	*Too-le-pan'*

I'd like a bouquet
Quería un ramo de flores
Keh-ree'-ah oon rah'-moh deh flau'-rehs

What are these flowers called?
¿Cómo se llaman estas flores?
Cau'-moh seh lyah'-man es'-tahs flau'-rehs?

Can you send it to this address before twelve tomorrow?
¿Pueden mandarlo a esta dirección mañana antes de las doce?
Pweh'-den man-dar'-loh ah es'-tah de-rec-thyon' mah-nyah'-nah an'-tes deh lahs dau'-theh?

Could you please send this card too?
Envíen también esta tarjeta, por favor
En-be'-en tam-byen' es'-tah tar-heh'-tah, paur fah-baur'

AT THE TOBACCONIST'S

Tobacconist's	Estanco	*Es-tan'-coh*
Tobacco	Tabaco	*Tah-bah'-coh*
Cigarette	Cigarrillo	*The-gar-ree'-lyoh*

Cigar	Puro	*Poo'-roh*
Matches	Cerillas	*Theh-ree'-lyahs*
Lighter	Encendedor/mechero	*En-then-deh-daur/*
		meh-cheh'-roh
Pipe	Pipa	*Pee'-pah*
Cigarette holder	Boquilla	*Bau-kee'-lyah*
Carton	Cartón	*Car-taun'*

Virginia/black/pipe tobacco
Tabaco rubio/negro/de pipa
Tah-bah'-coh roo'-byo/neh'-groh/deh pee'-pah

A packet of filter tipped cigarettes, please
Un paquete de cigarrillos con filtro, por favor
*Deh'-meh oon pah-keh'-teh deh the-gar-ree'-lyohs caun feel'-troh,
paur fah-baur'*

What type?
¿De qué marca?
Deh keh mar'-cah?

Give me a box of matches too
Deme también una caja de cerillas
Deh'-meh tam-byen' oo'-nah cah'-hah deh theh-ree'-lyahs

AT THE HAIRDRESSER'S

Hairdresser	Peluquero/a	*Peh-loo-keh'-roh/rah*
Hair	Pelo (cabello)	*Peh'-loh*
		(cah-beh'-lyoh)
Scissors	Tijeras	*Te-heh'-rahs*
Comb	Peine	*Pey-neh*
Brush	Cepillo	*Theh-pee'-lyoh*
Dryer	Secador	*Seh-cah-daur'*
Shampoo	Champú	*Cham-poo'*

Conditioner	Suavizante	*Swa-be-than'-teh*
Plait	Trenza	*Tren'-thah*
Fringe	Flequillo	*Fleh-kee'-lyoh*
Curl	Rizo	*Ree'-thoh*
Shampooing	Lavado	*Lah-bah'-doh*
Hair style	Peinado	*Pey-nah'-doh*
Highlights	Mechas	*Meh'-chahs*
Manicure	Manicura	*Mah-ne-coo'-rah*
Dyeing	Tinte	*Tin'-teh*

Anti-dranduff shampoo
Champú anticaspa
Cham-poo' an-te-cas'-pah

Hair cut
Corte de pelo
Caur'-teh deh peh'-loh

Shampoo and style
Lavar y peinar
Lah-bar' ee pey-nar'

The water is too hot/cold
El agua está demasiado caliente/fría
El ah'-gwa es-tah' deh-mah-sya'-doh cah-lyen'-teh/free'-ah

My hair is greasy/dry
Tengo el cabello graso/seco
Ten'-goh el cah-beh'-lyoh grah'-soh/seh'-coh

I'm losing a lot of hair
Se me cae mucho el pelo
Seh meh cah'-eh moo'-choh el peh'-loh

Trim the ends!
¡Córteme sólo las puntas!
Caur'-teh-meh sau'-loh lahs poon'-tahs!

I'd like a hair cut like this
Quiero un corte como éste
Kye'-roh oon caur'-teh cau'-moh es'-teh

I'd like to dye my hair/have a perm
Quisiera teñirme el pelo/hacerme un moldeador
*Ke-sye'-rah teh-nyeer'-meh el peh'-loh/ah-ther'-meh oon
maul-deh-ah-daur'*

Same colour?
¿Del mismo color?
Dehl mees'-moh cau-laur'?

A little darker/lighter
Un poco más oscuro/claro
*Oon pau'-coh mas aus-coo'-roh/
mas clah'-roh*

How shall I set your hair?
¿Cómo la peino?
Cau'-moh lah pey-noh?

Towards the back, without any parting
Todo hacia atrás, sin raya
Tau'-doh ah'-thya ah-tras', sin rah'-yah

That's fine, thank you
Así está bien, gracias
Ah-see' es-tah' byen, grah'-thyas

How much is that?
¿Cuánto le debo?
Kwan'-toh leh deh'-boh?

MEN'S HAIRDRESSER

Shave	Afeitado	*Ah-fey-tah'-doh*
Beard	Barba	*Bar'-bah*
Moustache	Bigote	*Be-gau'-teh*
Sideboards	Patillas	*Pah-tee'-lyahs*

I want a shave
Deseo afeitarme
Deh-seh'-oh ah-fey-tar'-meh

Trim the moustache
Arrégleme el bigote
Ar-reh'-gleh-meh el be-gau'-teh

A razor cut, please
Córteme el pelo a navaja
*Caur'-teh-meh el peh'-loh ah
nah-bah'-hah*

Just a trim
No me corte mucho
Noh meh caur'-teh moo'-choh

LEISURE

What places of interest are there in the town?
¿Qué lugares de interés hay en la ciudad?
Keh' loo-gah'-rehs deh in-teh-rehs' ah'-y en lah thew-dad'?

Monument	Monumento	*Mau-noo-men'-toh*
Museum	Museo	*Moo-seh'-oh*
Art gallery	Galería de arte	*Gah-leh-ree'-ah deh ar'-teh*
Cathedral	Catedral	*Cah-teh-drahl'*
Church	Iglesia	*E-gleh'-sya*
Chapel	Capilla	*Cah-pee'-lyah*
Cloister	Claustro	*Clah'-oos-troh*
Dome	Cúpula	*Coo'-poo-lah*
Nave	Nave	*Nah'-beh*
Palace	Palacio	*Pah-lah'-thyo*
Tower	Torre	*Taur'-reh*
Courtyard	Patio	*Pah'-tyo*

MUSEUMS AND ART GALLERIES

Visiting hours	Horas de visita	*Au'-ras deh be-se'-tah*
Open	Abierto	*Ah-byer'-toh*
Closed	Cerrado	*Ther-rah'-doh*
Free admission	Entrada libre	*En-trah'-dah lee'-breh*

Ticket	Entrada	*En-trah'-dah*
Brochure	Catálogo	*Cah-tah'-lau-goh*
Gift shop	Tienda de regalos	*Tyen'-dah deh reh-gah'-lohs*
Cloakroom	Guardarropa	*Gwar-dar-rau'-pah*
Halls	Salas	*Sah'-lahs*
Exhibition	Exposición	*Ex-pau-se-thyon'*
Guide	Guía	*Ghee'-ah*
Drawing	Dibujo	*De-boo'-hoh*
Engraving	Grabado	*Grah-bah'-doh*
Pottery	Cerámica	*Theh-rah'-me-cah*
Sculpture	Escultura	*Es-cool-too'-rah*
Watercolour	Acuarela	*Ah-kwa-reh'-lah*
Portrait	Retrato	*Reh-trah'-toh*
Landscape	Paisaje	*Pah-e-sah'-heh*

Picture
Cuadro (pintura)
Kwa'-droh (pin-too'-rah)

Classical paintings
Pintura clásica
Pin-too'-rah clah'-se-cah

Modern art
Arte moderno
Ar'-teh moh-der'-noh

Impressionist paintings
Pintura impresionista
Pin-too'-rah im-preh-syo-nees'-tah

Oil painting
Pintura al óleo
Pin-too'-rah ahl au'-leh-oh

No photography
Prohibido hacer fotografías
Proy-bee'-doh ah-ther' fau-tau-grah-fee'-ahs

What time does the Fine Arts Museum open/close?
¿A qué hora abre/cierra el Museo de Bellas Artes?
Ah keh' au'-rah ah'-breh/thyer'-rah el moo-seh'-oh deh beh'-lyahs ar'-tehs?

The museum is closed on Mondays
El museo cierra los lunes
El moo-seh'-oh thyer'-rah lohs loo'-nehs

Is there an admission charge?
¿Hay que pagar por entrar?
Ah'-y keh pah-gar' paur en-trar'?

Only for the exhibition
Sólo por la exposición
Sau'-loh paur lah ex-pau-se-thyon'

What time does the next guided tour start?
¿A qué hora es la siguiente visita guiada?
Ah keh' au'-rah es lah se-ghyen'-teh be-see'-tah ghya'-dah?

Would you like an audio-guide?
¿Quieren una audio-guía?
Kye'-ren oo'-nah ow-dyo-ghee'-ah?

Do you have a plan of the museum?
¿Tienen algún plano del museo?
Tye'-nen al-goon' plah'-noh dehl moo-seh'-oh?

Who is this painting by?
¿Quién lo pintó?
Kyen' loh pin-toh'?

ENTERTAINMENTS

BUYING TICKETS

Ticket office	Venta de entradas	*Ben'-tah deh en-trah'-dahs*
Box office	Taquilla	*Tah-kee'-lyah*
Ticket	Entrada	*En-trah'-dah*
Row	Fila	*Fee'-lah*
Seat	Asiento	*Ah-syen'-toh*

Do we need to book?
¿Hay que reservar?
Ah'-y keh reh-ser-bar'?

I'd like two tickets for tomorrow night/next Friday

Quisiera dos entradas para mañana por la noche/el viernes próximo

Ke-sye'-rah daus en-trah'-dahs pah'-rah mah-nyah'-nah paur lah nau'-cheh/el byer'-nehs prauc'-se-moh

What tickets do you have available?

¿Qué entradas hay disponibles?

Keh en-trah'-dahs ah'-y dis-poh-nee'-blehs?

I'm sorry, it's fully booked

Lo siento, está todo completo

Loh se-ehn'-toh, es-tah' tau'-doh caum-pleh'-toh

How much are the tickets?

¿Cuánto valen las entradas?

Kwan'-toh bah'-len lahs en-trah'-dahs?

Is there a discount for senior citizens/students?

¿Hay algún descuento para mayores/estudiantes?

Ah'-y al-goon' des-kwen'-toh pah'-rah mah-yoh'-rehs/es-too-dyan'-tes?

Can I pay by credit card?

¿Puedo pagar con tarjeta?

Pweh'-doh pah-gar' caun tar-heh'-tah?

What is your card number?

¿Cuál es su número de tarjeta?

Kwal' es soo noo'-meh'-roh deh tar-heh'-tah?

What is the expiry date?

¿Cuál es la fecha de caducidad?

Kwal' es lah feh'-chah deh cah-doo-the-dad'?

When do I collect the tickets?

¿Cuándo puedo recoger las entradas?

Kwan'-doh pweh'-doh reh-cau-her' lahs en-trah'-dahs?

AT THE THEATRE

Theatre	Teatro	Teh-ah'-troh
Play	Obra	Au'-brah
Actor	Actor	Ac-taur'
Actress	Actriz	Ac-treeth'
Aisle	Pasillo	Pah-see'-lyoh
Stalls	Platea	Plah-teh'-ah
Boxes	Palcos	Pahl'-cohs
Stage	Escenario	Es-theh-nah'-ryo
Scenery	Decorados	Deh-cau-rah'-dohs
Show	Función	Foon-thyon'
Act	Acto	Ac'-toh
Interval	Entreacto	En-treh-ac'-toh

What is on at the Theatre ... tonight?
¿Qué ponen en el Teatro ... esta noche?
Keh' pau'-nen en el teh-ah'-troh ... es'-tah nau-cheh?

When is the play on until?
¿Hasta cuándo estará la obra en cartel?
As'-tah kwan'-doh es-tah-rah' lah au'-brah en car-tehl'?

What time does the performance start?
¿A qué hora empieza la obra?
Ah keh' au'-rah em-pye'-thah lah au'-brah?

How long does the performance last?
¿Cuánto dura?
Kwan'-toh doo'-rah?

Could I have a programme, please?
¿Podría darme un programa, por favor?
Pau-dree'-ah dar'-meh oon prau-grah'-mah, paur fah-baur'?

Where is the cloakroom?
¿Dónde está el guardarropa?
Daun'-deh es-tah' el gwar-dar-rau'-pah?

CONCERTS

Concert hall	Sala de conciertos	*Sah'-lah deh caun-thyer'-tohs*
Opera house	Ópera	*Oh'-peh-rah*
Music	Música	*Moo'-se-cah*
Musician	Músico	*Moo'-se-coh*
Orchestra	Orquesta	*Aur-kes'-tah*
Conductor	Director	*De-rec-taur'*
Singer	Cantante	*Can-tan'-teh*
Audience	Público	*Poo'-ble-coh*

AT THE CINEMA

Cinema	Cine	*Thee'-neh*
List of plays	Cartelera	*Car-teh-leh'-rah*
Film	Película	*Peh-lee'-coo-lah*
Screen	Pantalla	*Pan-tah'-lyah*
Showing	Sesión	*Seh-syon'*
Documentary	Documental	*Dau-coo-men-tahl'*
Cartoons	Dibujos animados	*De-boo'-hohs ah-ne-mah'-dohs*

What's on at the … cinema?
¿Qué echan en el cine …?
Keh eh'-chan en el thee'-neh …?

Where is the new film by ... on?
¿Dónde se proyecta la nueva película de ...?
Daun'-deh seh prau-yec'-tah lah nweh'-bah peh-lee'-coo-lah deh...?

Is it in the original language with subtitles?
¿Es en versión original con subtítulos?
Es en ber'-syon' au-re-ge-nahl' caun soob-tee'-too-lohs?

No, it's dubbed
No, está doblada
Noh, es-tah' dau-blah'-dah

At a Nightclub

Do you know any good clubs near here?
¿Hay una buena discoteca cerca de aquí?
Ah'-y oo'-nah bweh'-nah dis-coh-teh'-cah ther'-cah deh ah-kee'?

What time do you close?
¿A qué hora cierran?
Ah keh' au'-rah thyer'-ran?

Do you have any live music tonight?
¿Tienen música en vivo esta noche?
Tye'-nen moo'-se-cah en bee'-boh es'-tah nau'-cheh?

On the beach/At the swimming pool

Beach	Playa	*Plah'-yah*
Sea	Mar	*Mar*
Swimming pool	Piscina	*Pis-thee'-nah*
Sand	Arena	*Ah-reh'-nah*
Wave	Ola	*Au'-lah*
Shore	Orilla	*Au-ree'-lyah*
Boat	Barca	*Bar'-cah*
Sunshade	Sombrilla	*Saum-bree'-lyah*
Sun bed	Tumbona	*Toom-bau'-nah*
Bathing costume	Bañador	*Bah-nyah-daur'*
Spring board	Trampolín	*Tram-pau-leen'*
Shower	Ducha	*Doo'-chah*

Is it dangerous to swim here?
¿Es peligroso bañarse aquí?
Es peh-lee-grau'-soh bah-nyar'-seh ah-kee'?

Are there lifeguards?
¿Hay socorristas?
Ah'-y sau-caur-rees'-tahs?

The water is dirty (polluted)
El agua está sucia (contaminada)
El ah'-gwa es-tah' soo'-thya (caun-tah-me-nah'-dah)

CAMPING

Camp site	Camping	*Cahm'-pin*
Caravan	Caravana	*Cah-rah-bah'-nah*
Hammer	Martillo	*Mar-tee'-lyoh*
Lamp	Linterna	*Lin-ter'-nah*
Tin-opener	Abrelatas	*Ah-breh-lah'-tahs*
Pocket knife	Navaja	*Nah-bah'-hah*
Corkscrew	Sacacorchos	*Sah-cah-caur'-chohs*
Toilets	Servicios	*Ser-bee'-thyos*

Tent	**Sleeping bag**
Tienda de campaña	Saco de dormir
Tyen'-dah deh cam-pah'-nyah	*Sah'-coh deh daur-meer'*

Butane cylinder	**Power point**
Bombona de butano	Enchufe
Baum-bau'-nah deh boo-tah'-noh	*En-choo'-feh*

I'm looking for a camp-site near the beach
Estoy buscando un camping cerca de la playa
Es-toy boos-can'-doh oon cahm'-pin ther'-cah deh lah plah'-yah

Can you tell me the daily fee?
¿Cuál es la tarifa diaria?
Kwal' es lah tah-ree'-fah dya'-rya?

We'd like to stay for ... days
Queremos quedarnos ... días
Keh-reh'-mohs keh-dar'-nohs ... dee'-ahs

Can we pitch the tent here?
¿Podemos montar la tienda aquí?
Pau-deh'-mohs maun-tar' lah tyen'-dah ah-kee'?

Where can I park my car?
¿Dónde puedo aparcar el coche?
Daun'-deh pweh'-doh ah-par-car' el cau'-cheh?

Is the water drinkable?
¿Es agua potable?
Es ah'-gwa pau-tah'-bleh?

Can we light a fire?
¿Podemos encender fuego?
Pau-deh'-mohs en-then-der' fweh'-goh?

Is there a night watchman on the camp-site?
¿Hay vigilancia nocturna?
Ah'-y be-he-lan'-thya nauc-toor'-nah?

Is there a supermarket near here?
¿Hay un supermercado cerca?
Ah'-y oon soo-per-mer-cah'-doh ther'-cah?

SPORTS

Where is the nearest ...?
¿Dónde está el/la ... más próximo/a?
Daun'-deh es-tah' el/lah ... mas prauc'-se-moh/ah?

gym	gimnasio	*him-nah'-syo*
swimming pool	piscina	*pis-thee'-nah*

sports centre
polideportivo
pau-le-deh-paur-tee'-boh

tennis court
pista de tenis
pees'-tah deh teh'-nihs

golf course
campo de golf
cahm'-poh deh gaulf

football ground
campo de fútbol
cahm'-poh deh foot'-baul

I'd like to hire a sailboard
Quería alquilar una tabla de windsurfing
Keh-ree'-ah al-ke-lar' oo'-nah tah'-blah deh windsurfing

How much does a one-hour lesson cost?
¿Cuánto cuesta una hora de clase?
Kwan'-toh kwes'-tah oo'-nah au'-rah deh clah'-seh?

I'd like to book the court for tomorrow at ...
Quisiera reservar la pista para mañana a las ...
Ke-sye'-rah reh-ser-bar' lah pees'-tah pah'-rah mah-nyah'-nah ah lahs ...

USEFUL SERVICES

Bank	Banco	*Ban'-coh*
Savings bank	Caja de ahorros	*Cah'-hah deh ah-aur'-rohs*
Exchange	Cambio	*Cahm'-byo*
Exchange rate	Cotización	*Cau-te-thah-thyon'*
Foreign currency	Divisas	*De-bee'-sahs*
Interest rate	Interés	*In-teh-res'*
Receipt	Recibo	*Reh-thee'-boh*
Money	Dinero	*De-neh'-roh*
Coin	Moneda	*Mau-neh'-dah*
Note	Billete	*Be-lyeh'-teh*
Pound	Libra	*Lee'-brah*
Dollar	Dólar	*Dau'-lar*
Euro	Euro	*Eh'-oo-roh*
Cent	Céntimo	*Then'-te-moh*
Cheque	Cheque	*Cheh'-keh*
Counter	Ventanilla	*Ben-tah-nee'-lyah*
Cashier's desk	Caja	*Cah'-hah*
Bank transfer	Transferencia	*Trans-feh-ren'-thya*
Bank charges	Comisión	*Cau-mee-syon'*
To pay in	Ingresar	*In-greh-sar'*
To withdraw	Sacar/retirar	*Sah-car'/reh-te-rar'*

Current account

Cuenta corriente

Kwehn'-tah caur-ryen'-teh

Cash dispenser

Cajero automático

Cah-heh'-roh ow-tau-mah'-te-coh

Traveller's cheque

Cheque de viaje

Cheh'-keh deh bya'-heh

Credit card

Tarjeta de crédito

Tar-heh'-tah deh creh'-de-toh

What are the banking hours?

¿Cuál es el horario de los bancos?

Kwal' es el au-rah'-ryo deh lohs ban'-cohs?

I'd like to withdraw ... euros, please

Quisiera sacar ... euros, por favor

Ke-sye'-rah sah-car'... eh'-oo-rohs, paur fah-baur'

Do you have any identification?

¿Tiene algún tipo de identificación?

Tye'-neh al-goon' tee'-poh deh e-den-te-fe-cah-thyon'?

How would you like the money?

¿Cómo quiere el dinero?

Cau'-moh kye'-reh el de-neh'-roh?

Could you give me some smaller notes?

¿Podría darme algunos billetes pequeños, por favor?

Pau-dree'-ah dar'-meh ahl-goo'-nohs be-lyeh'-tehs peh-keh'-nyohs, paur fah-baur'?

I'd like to pay this into my account, please

Quiero ingresar esto en mi cuenta, por favor

Kye'-roh in-greh-sar' es'-toh en mee kwehn'-tah, paur fah-baur'

Could you tell me my balance, please?

¿Podría decirme mi saldo, por favor?

Pau-dree'-ah deh-theer'-meh mee sahl'-doh, paur fah-baur'?

What is your bank account, please?
¿Cuál es su número de cuenta, por favor?
Kwal' es soo noo'-meh'-roh deh kwehn'-tah, paur fah-baur'?

I'd like to change some money
Quería cambiar dinero
Keh-ree'-ah cam-be-ar' de-neh'-roh

What is the exchange rate for euros?
¿A cómo está el cambio en euros?
A cau'-moh es-tah' el cahm'-byo en eh'-oo-rohs?

Can I cash this bearer cheque?
¿Puedo cobrar este cheque al portador?
Pweh'-doh cau-brar' es'-teh cheh'-keh ahl paur-tah-daur'?

Sign here, please
Firme aquí, por favor
Feer'-meh ah-kee', paur fah-baur'

Go to the cashier's desk (counter number ...)
Pase por caja (ventanilla número ...)
Pah'-seh paur cah'-hah (ben-tah-nee'-lyah noo'-meh-roh ...)

CASH DISPENSERS

Where is the nearest cash dispenser?
¿Hay un cajero automático cerca de aquí?
Ah'-y oon cah-heh'-roh ow-tau-mah'-te-coh ther'-cah deh ah-kee'?

Insert your card
Introduzca su tarjeta
In-ser'-teh soo tar-heh'-tah

Enter your PIN
Introduzca su número secreto
In-trau-dooth'-cah soo noo'-meh-roh seh-creh'-toh

Withdraw cash
Sacar dinero
Sah-car' de-neh'-roh

Other amount
Otras cantidades
Au'-trahs can-te-dah'-dehs

Enter/Correct/Cancel
Aceptar/Corregir/Cancelar
Ah-thep-tar'/caur-reh-heer'/can-theh-lar'

Another service?
¿Desea realizar otra operación?
Deh-seh'-ah reh-ah-le-thar' au'-trah au-peh-rah-thyon'?

Balance
Consultar saldo
Caun-sool-tar' sahld'-doh

Please, wait
Por favor, espere
Paur fah-baur', es-peh'-reh

Please take your card
Por favor, retire su tarjeta
Paur fah-baur', reh-tee'-reh soo tar-heh'-tah

AT THE POST OFFICE

Post office	Correos	*Caur-reh'-ohs*
Letter box	Buzón	*Boo-thaun'*
By mail	Por correo	*Paur caur-reh'-oh*
Air mail	Por avión	*Paur ah-byon'*
Delivery	Envío	*En-bee'-oh*
Collection	Recogida	*Reh-cau-hee'-dah*
Letter	Carta	*Car'-tah*
Postcard	Postal	*Paus-tahl'*
Stamp	Sello	*Seh'-lyoh*

Address	Dirección	*De-rec-thyon'*
Sender	Remitente	*Reh-me-ten'-teh*
Addressee	Destinatario	*Des-te-nah-tah'-ryo*
Parcel	Paquete	*Pah-keh'-teh*
Envelope	Sobre	*Sau'-breh*

Padded bag
Sobre acolchado
Sau'-breh ah-caul-chah'-doh

Poste restante
Lista de correos
Lees'-tah deh caur-reh'-ohs

Postal code
Código postal
Cau'-de-goh paus-tahl'

P.O. Box
Apartado de correos
Ah-par-tah'-doh deh caur-reh'-ohs

Recorded letter
Carta certificada
Car'-tah ther-te-fe-cah'-dah

Express
Urgente
Oor-hen'-teh

Printed matter
Impresos
Im-preh'-sohs

Cash on delivery
Contra reembolso
Caun'-trah reh-em-baul'-soh

Is there a letter box near here?
¿Dónde hay un buzón?
Daun'-deh ah'-y oon boo-thaun'?

What time is the post office open?
¿A qué hora abre Correos?
Ah keh' au'-rah ah'-breh caur-reh'-os?

I need a stamp for Europe
Un sello para Europa
Oon seh'-lyoh pah'-rah eh-oo-roh'-pah

Which counter is for registered mail?
¿Cuál es la ventanilla de Certificados?
Kwal' es lah ben-tah-nee'-lyah deh ther-te-fe-cah'-dohs?

I'd like to send this letter by express mail

Quisiera enviar esta carta urgente

Ke-sye'-rah en-be-ar' es'-tah car'-tah oor-hen'-teh

How much will it cost to send this parcel to ...?

¿Cuánto me costaría enviar este paquete a ...?

Kwan'-toh meh caus-tah-ree'-ah en-byar' es'-teh pah-keh'-teh ah ...?

What documents do I need to collect a parcel?

¿Qué documentos necesito para recoger un paquete?

Keh' dau-coo-men'-tohs ne-theh-see'-toh pah'-rah reh-cau-her' oon pah-keh'-teh?

Can you fill in this form, please?

¿Podría rellenar este impreso, por favor?

Pau-dree'-ah reh-lyeh-nar' es'-teh im-preh'-soh, paur fah-baur'?

Put today's date and sign here, please

Ponga la fecha de hoy y firme aquí, por favor

Paun'-gah lah feh'-chah deh oy ee feer'-meh ah-kee', paur fah-baur'

I'd like to cash this postal order

Deseo cobrar este giro postal

Deh-seh'-oh cau-brar' es'-teh hee'-roh paus-tahl'

Public telephone	Teléfono público	*Teh-leh'-fau-noh*
		poo'-ble-coh
Telephone box	Cabina	*Cah-bee'-nah*
Call centre	Locutorio	*Loh-coo-toh'-ryo*
Coins	Monedas	*Mau-neh'-dahs*
Number	Número	*Noo'-meh-roh*
Code number	Prefijo	*Preh-fee'-hoh*
Telephone call	Llamada	*Lyah-mah'-dah*
Message	Mensaje	*Men-sah'-heh*

Directory enquiries
Información telefónica
In-faur-ma-thyon'
teh-leh-fau'-ne-cah

White/yellow pages
Páginas blancas/amarillas
Pah'-he-nahs blan'-cahs/
ah-mah-ree'-lyas

Answering machine
Contestador
Caun-tes-tah-daur'

Telephone directory
Guía telefónica
Ghee'-ah teh-leh-fau'-ne-cah

Fixed line
Teléfono fijo
Teh-leh'-fau-noh fee'-hoh

Mobile phone/Cellphone
(Teléfono) móvil
(Teh-leh'-fau-noh) mau'-beel

Phonecard
Tarjeta de teléfono
Tar-heh'-tah deh teh-leh'-fau-noh

Prepaid card
Tarjeta de prepago
Tar-heh'-tah deh preh-pah'-goh

I'd like to make a collect call to ...
Quiero hacer una llamada a cobro revertido a ...
Kye'-roh ah-ther' oo'-nah lyah-mah'-dah ah cau'-broh reh-ber-tee'-doh ah ...

What is the code for ...?
¿Cuál es el prefijo de ...?
Kwal' es el preh-fee'-hoh deh ...?

The number is not working
El número marcado no existe
El noo'-meh-roh mar-cah'-doh noh ec-sees'-teh

There is no answer
No contestan
Noh caun-tehs'-tan

It's engaged
Está comunicando
Es-tah' cau-moo-ne-can'-doh

Hello!
¡Dígame!
Dee'-gah-meh!

This is ...
Soy ...
Soy ...

Could I speak to ..., please?
¿Podría hablar con ...?
Pau-dree'-ah ah-blar' caun ...?

Speaking
Soy yo
Soy yoh

Who is calling?
¿De parte de quién?
Deh par'-teh deh kyen'?

You have got the wrong number
Se ha equivocado
Seh ah eh-ke-bau-cah'-doh

Just a moment, please
Un momento, por favor
Oon mau-men'-toh, paur fah-baur'

Hold the line
No cuelgue
Noh kwehl'-gheh

I'll put him/her on
Le paso con él/ella
Leh pah'-soh caun ehl/eh'-lyah

He/she is out
Ha salido
Ah sah-lee'-doh

Would you like to leave a message?
¿Quiere dejarle un recado?
Kye'-reh deh-har'-leh oon reh-cah'-doh?

Tell him/her that ... has called
Dígale que ... ha llamado
Dee'-gah-leh keh ... ah lyah-mah'-doh

I'll call back later
Llamaré más tarde
Lyah-mah-reh' mas tar'-deh

Thanks for calling
Gracias por su llamada
Grah'-thyas paur soo lyah-mah'-dah

ANSWERING MACHINE

There is no-one here to take your call at the moment
En estos momentos no podemos atenderle
En es'-tohs moh-men'-tohs noh poh-deh'-mos ah-ten-der'-leh

Please, leave your message after the beep
Por favor, deje su mensaje después de la señal
Paur fah-baur', deh'-heh soo men-sah'-heh des-pwes' deh lah seh-nyahl'

MOBILE PHONES

I need to charge up my phone
Necesito recargar mi móvil
Neh-theh-see'-toh reh-car-gar' mee mau'-beel

My battery is about to run out
Se me va a acabar pronto la batería
Seh meh bah ah ah-cah-bar' praun'-toh lah bah-teh-ree'-ah

I'm about to run out of credit
Voy a quedarme sin saldo
Boh'-y ah keh-dar'-meh sin sahl'-doh

I'll send you a text message
Te enviaré un mensaje de texto
Teh en-bya-reh' oon men-sah'-heh deh tex'-toh

FAX

Could I send a fax?
¿Podría enviar un fax?
Pau-dree'-ah en-be-ar' oon fax?

How much is per page?
¿Cuánto cuesta cada hoja?
Kwan'-toh kwes'-tah cah'-dah au'-hah?

INTERNET

Internet access	**E-mail**
Conexión a internet	Correo electrónico
Coh-nec-syon' ah in-ter-net'	*Caur-reh'-oh eh-lec-trau'-ne-coh*

What are your prices for Internet access?
¿Cuáles son las tarifas de internet?
Kwa'-lehs saun lahs tah-ree'-fahs deh in-ter-net'?

What is your e-mail address?
¿Cuál es su dirección de correo electrónico?
Kwal' es soo de-rec-thyon' deh caur-reh'-oh eh-lec-trau'-ne-coh?

I'm sending it as an attachment in an e-mail
Le envío el documento por correo electrónico
Leh en-bee'-oh el doh-coo-men'-toh paur caur roh' oh eh-lec-trau'-ne-coh

Police station	Comisaría	*Cau-me-sah-ree'-ah*
Police	Policía	*Pau-le-thee'-ah*
Police officer	Policía	*Pau-le-thee'-ah*
Report	Denuncia	*Deh-noon'-thya*
Statement	Declaración	*Deh-clah-rah-thyon'*
Lawyer	Abogado	*Ah-bau-gah'-doh*
Theft	Robo	*Rau'-boh*
Thief	Ladrón	*Lah-draun'*
Mugging	Atraco	*Ah-trah'-coh*
Aggression	Agresión	*Ah-greh-syon'*
Fight	Pelea	*Peh-leh'-ah*
Accident	Accidente	*Ac-the-den'-teh*
Witness	Testigo	*Tes-tee'-goh*
Passport	Pasaporte	*Pah-sah-paur'-teh*
Wallet	Cartera	*Car-teh'-rah*
Handbag	Bolso	*Baul'-soh*

Where is the nearest police station?
¿Dónde está la comisaría más próxima?
Daun'-deh es-tah' lah cau-me-sah-ree'-ah mas prauc'-se-mah?

My ... has been stolen
Me han robado el/la ...
Meh an rau-bah'-doh el/lah ...

I've been hit
Me han golpeado
Meh an gaul-peh-ah'-doh

I've lost my passport

Se me ha perdido el pasaporte

Seh meh ah per-dee'-doh el pah-sah-paur'-teh

I've had a car accident

He tenido un accidente de coche

Eh teh-nee'-doh oon ac-the-den'-teh deh cau'-cheh

I don't understand. Can I have an interpreter?

No entiendo. ¿Puede venir un intérprete?

Noh en-tyen'-doh. Pweh'-doh beh-neer' oon in-ter'-preh-teh?

Can I call my embassy/consulate?

¿Puedo llamar a mi embajada/consulado?

Pweh'-doh lyah-mar' ah mee em-bah-hah'-dah/caun-soo-lah'-doh?

How should I fill in the report?

¿Cómo debo cumplimentar la denuncia?

Cau'-moh deh'-boh coom-ple-men-tar' lah deh-noon'-thya?

Please complete and sign this form

Rellene este impreso y firmelo

Reh-lyeh-neh' es'-teh im-preh'-soh ee feer'-meh-loh

HEALTH

Head	Cabeza	*Cah-beh'-thah*
Face	Cara	*Cah'-rah*
Eye	Ojo	*Au'-hoh*
Nose	Nariz	*Nah-reeth'*
Ear	Oído/oreja	*Au-ee'-doh/ au-reh'-hah*
Mouth	Boca	*Bau'-cah*
Tongue	Lengua	*Len'-gwa*
Throat	Garganta	*Gar-gan'-tah*
Neck	Cuello	*Kweh'-lyoh*
Shoulder	Hombro	*Aum'-broh*
Arm	Brazo	*Brah'-thoh*
Elbow	Codo	*Cau'-doh*
Wrist	Muñeca	*Moo-nyeh'-cah*
Hand	Mano	*Mah'-noh*
Finger	Dedo	*Deh'-doh*
Back	Espalda	*Es-pahl'-dah*
Chest	Pecho	*Peh'-choh*
Leg	Pierna	*Pyer'-nah*
Knee	Rodilla	*Rau-dee'-lyah*
Foot	Pie	*Pye'*
Toe	Dedo del pie	*Deh'-doh dehl pye'*
Heart	Corazón	*Cau-rah-thaun'*

Stomach	Estómago	*Es-tau'-mah-goh*
Abdomen	Vientre	*Byen'-treh*
Lung	Pulmón	*Pool-maun'*
Liver	Hígado	*Ee'-gah-doh*
Kidneys	Riñones	*Re-nyau'-nehs*
Intestines	Intestinos	*In-tes-tee'-nohs*
Bone	Hueso	*Weh'-soh*

AT THE DOCTOR'S

Hospital	Hospital	*Aus-pe-tahl'*
Doctor	Médico	*Meh'-de-coh*
Nurse	Enfermera	*En-fer-meh'-rah*
Patient	Paciente	*Pah-thyen'-teh*
Illness	Enfermedad	*En-fer-meh-dad'*
Pain	Dolor	*Dau-laur'*
X-ray	Rayos X	*Rah'-yohs eh'-kis*
Prescription	Receta	*Reh-theh'-tah*

First aid
Primeros auxilios
Pre-meh'-rohs ow-xee'-lyos

Health centre
Centro de salud
Then'-troh deh sah-lood'

Private medical insurance
Seguro médico privado
*Seh-goo'-roh meh'-de-coh
pre-bah'-doh*

Health Insurance Card
Tarjeta sanitaria
Tar-heh'-tah sah-ne-tah'-rya

Surgery (room)
Consulta
Caun-sool'-tah

Waiting room
Sala de espera
Sah'-lah deh es-peh'-rah

Blood pressure
Presión sanguínea
Preh-syon' san-ghee'-neh-ah

Blood group
Grupo sanguíneo
Groo'-poh san-ghee'-neh-oh

Can you call a doctor?
¿Puede llamar a un médico?
Pweh'-deh lyah-mar' ah oon meh'-de-coh?

Do you know a doctor who speaks English?
¿Conoce a algún médico que hable inglés?
Cau-nau'-theh ah al-goon' meh'-de-coh keh ah'-bleh in-gles'?

Can you take me to the Casualty Department?
¿Puede llevarme a Urgencias?
Pweh'-deh lyeh-bar'-meh ah oor-hen'-thyas?

I don't feel well	**What is the matter?**
No me siento bien	¿Qué le pasa?
Noh meh syen'-toh byen	*Keh' leh pah'-sah?*

I've got ...
Tengo ...
Ten'-goh ...

flu (influenza)	gripe	*gree'-peh*
a cough	tos	*taus*
a temperature	fiebre	*fye'-breh*

a headache	**a stomach ache**
dolor de cabeza	dolor de estómago
dau-laur' deh cah-beh'-thah	*dau-laur' deh es-tau'-mah-goh*

a sore throat	**I've got a cold**
dolor de garganta	Estoy resfriado/a
dau-laur' deh gar-gan'-tah	*Es-toy res-frya'-doh/-dah*

I'm suffering from dizzy spells
Tengo mareos
Ten'-goh mah-reh'-ohs

I think I've broken my leg
Creo que me he roto una pierna
Creh'-oh keh meh eh rau'-toh oo'-nah pyer'-nah

I've sprained my ankle
Me he torcido un tobillo
Meh eh taur-thee'-doh oon tau-bee'-lyoh

I've difficulties in breathing
Me cuesta trabajo respirar
Meh kwes'-tah trah-bah'-hoh res-pe-rar'

I've heart problems
Padezco del corazón
Pah-deth'-coh dehl cau-rah-thaun'

Where does it hurt?
¿Dónde le duele?
Daun'-deh leh dweh'-leh?

How long have you been ill?
¿Desde cuándo está enfermo?
Des'-deh kwan'-doh es-tah' en-fer'-moh?

I'm allergic to ...
Soy alérgico/a a ...
Soy ah-ler'-he-coh/-ah ah ...

I'm in my ... week of pregnancy
Estoy embarazada de ... semanas
Es-toy em-bah-rah-thah'-dah deh ... seh-mah'-nahs

Are you on any sort of medication?
¿Está tomando alguna medicación?
Es-tah' tau-man'-doh ahl-goo'-nah meh-de-cah-thyon'?

Take a deep breath, cough, put out your tongue
Respire hondo, tosa, saque la lengua
Res-pee'-reh aun'-doh, tau'-sah, sah'-keh lah len'-gwa

Undress, please
Quítese la ropa, por favor
Kee'-teh-seh lah rau'-pah, paur fah-baur'

You need to rest
Debe guardar reposo
Deh'-beh gwar-dar' reh-pau'-soh

Don't worry
No se preocupe
Noh seh preh-au-coo'-peh

Take these pills/this syrup every ... hours
Tome estas pastillas/este jarabe cada ... horas
Tau'-meh es'-tahs pas-tee'-lyahs/es'-teh hah-rah'-beh cah'-dah ...
au'-rahs

Come back in ... days
Tiene que volver dentro de ... días
Tye'-neh keh baul-ber' den'-troh deh ... dee'-ahs

AT THE DENTIST'S

Teeth	Dientes	*Dyen'-tehs*
Back tooth	Muela	*Mweh'-lah*
Wisdom tooth	Muela del juicio	*Mweh'-lah dehl hoo-ee'-thyo*
Gum	Encía	*En-thee'-ah*
Tooth decay	Caries	*Cah'-ryes*
Filling	Empaste	*Em-pas'-teh*
Anaesthetic	Anestesia	*Ah-nes-teh'-sya*

This tooth hurts
Me duele este diente/muela
Meh dweh'-leh es'-teh dyen'-teh/mweh'-lah

I've a chipped tooth
Tengo una muela picada
Ten'-goh oo'-nah mweh'-lah pe-cah'-dah

I must take it out
Habrá que sacarla
Ah-brah' keh sah-car'-lah

I've lost a filling. Can you fill it at once?

Se me ha caído un empaste. ¿Puede empastármelo en seguida?

Seh meh ah cah-y'-doh oon em-pas'-teh. Pweh'-deh em-pas-tar'-meh-loh en seh-ghee'-dah?

I need a clean up/a check up

Quiero hacerme una limpieza/una revisión

Kye'-roh ah-ther'-meh oo'-nah lim-pye'-thah/oo'-nah reh-be-syon'

Don't close your mouth

No cierre la boca

Noh thyer'-reh lah bau'-cah

Spit and rinse, please

Escupa y enjuáguese

Es-coo'-pah ee en-hwa'-gheh-seh

Don't chew for a few hours

No mastique en unas horas

Noh mas-tee'-keh en oo'-nahs au'-rahs

TRAVEL DICTIONARY

ENGLISH-SPANISH

a

all. todo. *tau'-doh*

almost. casi. *cah'-se*

alone. solo/a. *sau'-loh/-ah*

already ya *yah*

also. también. *tam-byen'*

although. aunque. *ah'-oon-keh*

always. siempre. *syem'-preh*

ambulance. ambulancia.
am-boo-lahn'-thya

among. entre. *en'-treh*

and. y. *ee*

another. otro/a. *au'-troh/-ah*

answer. respuesta.
res-pwes'-tah

any. algún/a. *al-goon'/-nah*

apartment. apartamento.
ah-par-tah-men'-toh

apple. manzana.
man-thah'-nah

appointment. cita. *thee'-tah*

apricot. albaricoque.
al-bah-re-cau'-keh

April. abril. *ah-breel'*

arm. brazo. *brah'-thoh*

arrive. llegar. *lyeh-gar'*

arrival. llegada. *lyeh-gah'-dah*

as. como, cuando.
cau'-moh, kwan'-doh

ask. preguntar. *preh-goon-tar'*

at. en, a. *en, ah*

attention. atención.
ah-ten-thyon'

August. agosto. *ah-gaus'-toh*

autumn. otoño. *au-tau'-nyoh*

avenue. avenida.
ah-beh-nee'-dah

b

back. espalda, atrás.
es-pahl'-dah, ah-tras'

bad. malo. *mah'-loh*

banana. plátano. *plah'-tah-noh*

bank. banco. *bahn'-coh*

bath. baño. *bah'-nyoh*

bathroom. cuarto de baño.
coo-ar'-toh deh bah'-nyoh

battery. pila, batería. *pee'-lah,
bah-teh-ree'-ah*

be. ser. *ser*

beach. playa. *plah'-yah*

beautiful. bonito. *bau-nee'-toh*

because. porque. *paur'-keh*

bed. cama. *cah'-mah*

bedroom. dormitorio.
daur-me-tau'-ryo

beer. cerveza. *ther-beh'-thah*

before. antes. *ahn'-tehs*

begin. empezar. *em-peh-thar'*

behind. detrás. *deh-tras'*

believe. creer. *creh-er'*

belt. cinturón. *thin-too-raun'*

best, better. mejor. *meh-haur'*

between. entre. *en'-treh*

bicycle. bicicleta. *be-the-cleh'-tah*

big. grande. *grahn'-deh*

bill. cuenta. *kwen'-tah*

biscuit. galleta. *gah-lyeh'-tah*

bitter. amargo. *ah-mar'-goh*

black. negro. *neh'-groh*

blanket. manta. *mahn'-tah*

blond. rubio/a. *roo'-byo/-ah*

blood. sangre. *sahn'-greh*

blue. azul. *ah-thool'*

body. cuerpo. *kwer'-poh*

bone. hueso. *we'-soh*

book. libro. *lee'-broh*

boot. bota. *bau'-tah*

bottle. botella. *bau-teh'-lyah*

box. caja. *cah'-hah*

boy. chico. *chee'-coh*

boyfriend. novio. *noh'-byoh*

bread. pan. *pahn*

breakdown. avería. *ah-beh-ree'-ah*

breakfast. desayuno. *deh-sah-yoo'-noh*

bridge. puente. *pwen'-teh*

bring. traer. *trah-er'*

broken. roto. *rau'-toh*

brother. hermano. *er-mah'-noh*

brown. marrón. *mar-raun'*

brush. cepillo. *theh-pee'-lyoh*

building. edificio. *eh-de-fee'-thyo*

bull. toro. *tau'-roh*

but. pero. *peh'-roh*

butcher's. carnicería. *car-ne-theh-ree'-ah*

butter. mantequilla. *man-teh-kee'-lyah*

buy. comprar. *caum'-prar'*

by. por, de. *paur, deh*

C

cake. pastel, tarta. *pas-tehl', tar'-tah*

call. llamar, llamada. *lyah-mar', lyah-mah'-dah*

camera. cámara. *cah'-mah-rah*

can. poder, lata. *pau-der', lah'-tah*

car. coche. *cau'-cheh*

card. tarjeta. *tar-heh'-tah*

carrot. zanahoria. *thah-nah-au'-rya*

carry. llevar. *lyeh-bar'*

cash. cobrar, caja. *cau-brar', cah'-hah*

castle. castillo. *cas-tee'-lyoh*

cat. gato. *gah'-toh*

cathedral. catedral. *cah-teh-drahl'*

caution. cuidado. *kwi-dah'-doh*

centre. centro. *then'-troh*

century. siglo. *see'-gloh*

chair. silla. *see'-lyah*

change. cambiar, cambio. *cam-be-ar', cam'-byo*

cheap. barato. *bah-rah'-toh*

cheese. queso. *keh'-soh*

chemist's. farmacia. *far-mah'-thya*

cheque. cheque. *cheh'-keh*

cherry. cereza. *theh-reh'-thah*

chicken. pollo. *pau'-lyoh*

child. niño. *nee'-nyoh*

chocolate. chocolate. *chau-cau-lah'-teh*

church. iglesia. *e-gleh'-sya*

cigarette. cigarrillo. *the-gar-ree'-lyoh*

cinema. cine. *thee'-neh*

city. ciudad. *thew-dad'*

clean. limpio. *leem'-pyo*

clear. claro. *clah'-roh*

climate. clima. *klee'-mah*

clinic. clínica. *klee'-ne-cah*

close. cerrar, cerca. *ther-rar', thehr'-cah*

closed. cerrado. *ther-rah'-doh*

clothes. ropa. *rau'-pah*

cloud. nube. *noo'-beh*

coach. autocar. *ow-tau-car'*

coast. costa. *caus'-tah*

coat. abrigo. *ah-bree'-goh*

coffee. café. *cah-feh'*

coin. moneda. *mau-neh'-dah*

cold. frío. *free'-oh*

colour. color. *cau-laur'*

come. venir. *beh-neer'*

concert. concierto. *caun-thyer'-toh*

constipation. estreñimiento. *es-treh-nye-myen'-toh*

cool. fresco. *fres'-coh*

corn. maíz. *mah-eth'*

corner. esquina. *es-kee'-nah*

cost. costar. *caus-tar'*

cotton. algodón. *al-gau-daun'*

cough. tos. *taus*

counter. mostrador. *maus-trah-daur'*

country. país. *pah-ees'*

cousin. primo. *pree'-moh*

cream. nata. *nah'-tah*

credit. crédito. *creh'-de-toh*

cross. cruzar. *croo-thar'*

cup. taza. *tah'-thah*

customs. aduana. *ah-dwa'-nah*

cut. corte, cortar. *caur'-teh, caur-tar'*

d

daily. diario. *dya'-ryo*

danger. peligro. *peh-lee'-groh*

dark. oscuro. *aus-coo'-roh*

date. fecha. *feh'-chah*

daughter. hija. *ee'-hah*

day. día. *dee'-ah*

December. diciembre. *de-thyem'-breh*

deck. cubierta. *coo-byer'-tah*

delay. retraso. *reh-trah'-soh*

dentist. dentista. *den-tees'-tah*

departure. salida. *sah-lee'-dah*

dessert. postre. *paus'-treh*

dictionary. diccionario. *dic-thyo-nah'-ryo*

difficult. difícil. *de-fee'-theel*

dinner. comida, cena. *cau-mee'-dah, theh'-nah*

direct. directo. *de-rec'-toh*

dirty. sucio. *soo'-thyo*

discount. descuento. *des-kwen'-toh*

163

dish. plato. *plah'-toh*

district. barrio. *bar'-ryo*

disturb. molestar. *mau-les-tar'*

do. hacer. *ah-thehr'*

doctor. médico. *meh'-de-coh*

dog. perro. *per'-roh*

dollar. dólar. *dau'-lar*

door. puerta. *pwer'-tah*

down. abajo. *ah-bah'-hoh*

dress. vestirse, vestido.
bes-teer'-seh, bes-tee'-doh

drink. beber, bebida. *beh-ber',*
beh-bee'-dah

drive. conducir. *caun-doo-theer'*

dry. seco. *seh'-coh*

during. durante. *doo-rahn'-teh*

e

each. cada. *cah'-dah*

ear. oído, oreja. *oy'-doh,*
au-reh'-hah

early. temprano. *tem-prah'-noh*

earth. tierra. *tyer'-rah*

east. este. *es'-teh*

easy. fácil. *fah'-theel*

eat. comer. *cau-mer'*

egg. huevo. *we'-boh*

eight. ocho. *au'-choh*

eighty. ochenta. *au-chehn'-tah*

eleven. once. *aun'-theh*

embassy. embajada.
em-bah-hah'-dah

empty. vacío. *bah-thee'-oh*

end. fin, final. *feen, fe-nahl'*

engine. motor. *mau-taur'*

enough. bastante.
bas-tahn'-teh

entry (entrance). entrada.
en-trah'-dah

envelope. sobre. *sau'-breh*

euro. euro. *eh'-oo-roh*

evening. tarde, noche.
tar'-deh, nau'-cheh

every. cada. *cah'-dah*

example. ejemplo.
eh-hehm'-ploh

exchange. cambio. *cahm'-byo*

excuse. disculpar, perdonar.
dis-cool-par', per-dau-nar'

exhibition. exposición.
ex-pau-se-thyon'

exit. salida. *sah-lee'-dah*

eye. ojo. *au'-hoh*

f

face. cara. *cah'-rah*

family. familia. *fah-mee'-lya*

far. lejos. *leh'-hohs*

fare. tarifa. *tah-ree'-fah*

fast. rápido. *rah'-pe-doh*

father. padre. *pah'-dreh*

February. febrero.
feh-breh'-roh

few. pocos. *pau'-cohs*

field. campo. *cahm'-poh*

fifteen. quince. *keen'-theh*

fifty. cincuenta. *thin-kwen'-tah*

fill. llenar, empastar. *lyeh-nar',*
em-pas-tar'

film. película. *peh-lee'-coo-lah*

find. encontrar. *en-caun-trar'*

fine. bonito, multa.
bau-nee'-toh, mool'-tah

finger. dedo. *deh'-doh*

finish. terminar. *ter-me-nar'*

fire. fuego. *fwe'-goh*

first. primero. *pre-meh'-roh*

fish. pescado. *pes-cah'-doh*

five. cinco. *theen'-coh*

flavour. sabor. *sah-baur'*

flight. vuelo. *bwe'-loh*

floor. piso, planta. *pee'-soh, plahn'-tah*

flower. flor. *flaur*

follow. seguir. *seh-gheer'*

food. comida. *cau-mee'-dah*

foot. pie. *pye'*

for. para. *pah'-rah*

forbidden. prohibido. *prau-e-bee'-doh*

foreign(er). extranjero. *ex-tran-heh'-roh*

fork. tenedor. *teh-neh-daur'*

forget. olvidar. *aul-be-dar'*

forty. cuarenta. *kwa-ren'-tah*

fountain. fuente. *fwen'-teh*

four. cuatro. *kwa'-troh*

fourteen. catorce. *cah-taur'-theh*

free. libre, gratis. *lee'-breh, grah'-tis*

Friday. viernes. *byer'-nehs*

fried. frito. *free'-toh*

friend. amigo/a. *ah-mee'-goh/-ah*

from. de, desde. *deh, des'-deh*

fruit. fruta. *froo'-tah*

full. lleno. *lyeh'-noh*

g

gallon. galón. *gah-laun'* (4,5 l)

garden. jardín. *har-deen'*

garlic. ajo. *ah'-hoh*

gate. puerta. *pwer'-tah*

gentleman. caballero. *cah-bah-lyeh'-roh*

gift. regalo. *reh-gah'-loh*

girl. chica. *chee'-cah*

girlfriend. novia. *noh'-byah*

give. dar. *dar*

glad. contento. *caun-ten'-toh*

glass. vaso, cristal. *bah'-soh, cris-tahl'*

glasses. gafas. *gah'-fahs*

go. ir. *eer*

go out. salir. *sah-leer'*

gold. oro. *au'-roh*

good. bueno. *bweh'-noh*

goodbye. adiós. *ah-dyos'*

grape. uva. *oo'-bah*

great. gran, grande. *grahn, grahn'-deh*

green. verde. *ber'-deh*

grey. gris. *grees*

group. grupo. *groo'-poh*

guide. guía. *ghee'-ah*

h

hair. pelo. *peh'-loh*

half. mitad, medio. *me-tad', meh'-dyo*

ham. jamón. *hah-maun'*

hand. mano. *mah'-noh*

handbag. bolso. *baul'-soh*

happen. pasar, ocurrir. *pah-sar', au-coor-reer'*

happy. feliz. *feh-leeth'*

harbour. puerto. *pwer'-toh*

hat. sombrero. *saum-breh'-roh*

have. tener, haber. *teh-ner', ah-ber'*

have lunch. almorzar. *al-maur-thar'*

he. él. *el*

head. cabeza. *cah-beh'-thah*

health. salud. *sah-lood'*

hear. oír. *oyr'*

heart. corazón. *cau-rah-thaun'*

help. ayudar, socorro. *ah-yoo-dar', sau-caur'-roh*

her. su, la, le. *soo, lah, leh*

high. alto. *ahl'-toh*

him. lo, le. *lau, leh*

hire. alquilar. *al-ke-lar'*

his. su. *soo*

holidays. vacaciones. *bah-cah-thyo'-nes*

home. casa, hogar. *cah'-sah, au-gar'*

honey. miel. *myel'*

hope. esperar. *es-peh-rar'*

hospital. hospital. *aus-pe-tahl'*

hot. caliente. *cah-lyen'-teh*

hotel. hotel. *au-tehl'*

hour. hora. *au'-rah*

house. casa. *cah'-sah*

how. cómo. *cau'-moh*

hunger. hambre. *ahm'-breh*

hurry. prisa. *pree'-sah*

hurt. herida, daño. *eh-ree'-dah, dah'-nyoh*

husband. marido. *mah-ree'-doh*

i

ice. hielo. *ye'-loh*

ice cream. helado. *eh-lah'-doh*

if. si. *see*

ill. enfermo/a. *en-fer'-moh/-ah*

in. en, dentro de. *en, den'-troh deh*

inch. pulgada. *pool-gah'-dah* (2,5 cm)

included. incluido. *in-clwi'-doh*

influenza. gripe. *gree'-peh*

injured. herido. *eh-ree'-doh*

interest. interés. *in-teh-res'*

interesting. interesante. *in-teh-reh-sahn'-teh*

interpreter. intérprete. *in-ter'-preh-teh*

introduce. presentar. *preh-sen-tar'*

invite. invitar. *in-bee-tar'*

island. isla. *ees'-lah*

it. lo. *loh*

j

jacket. chaqueta. *chah-keh'-tah*

jam. mermelada. *mer-meh-lah'-dah*

January. enero. *eh-neh'-roh*

jeans. vaqueros. *bah-keh'-rohs*

jewel. joya. *hau'-yah*

jeweller's. joyería. *hau-yeh-ree'-ah*

journey. viaje. *bya'-heh*

juice. zumo. *thoo'-moh*

July. julio. *hoo'-lyo*

June. junio. *hoo'-nyo*

k

key. llave. *lyah'-beh*

kidney. riñón. *re-nyaun'*

kind. tipo, amable. *tee'-poh, ah-mah'-bleh*

kitchen. cocina. *cau-thee'-nah*

knee. rodilla. *rau-dee'-lyah*

knife. cuchillo. *coo-chee'-lyoh*

know. saber, conocer. *sah-ber', cau-nau-thehr'*

l

lady. señora. *seh-nyau'-rah*

lake. lago. *lah'-goh*

lamp. lámpara. *lahm'-pah-rah*

land. tierra, aterrizar. *tyer'-rah, ah-ter-re-thar'*

language. lengua, idioma. *len'-gwa, e-dyo'-mah*

large. grande. *grahn'-deh*

last. último. *ool'-te-moh*

last night. anoche. *ah-nau'-cheh*

late. tarde. *tar'-deh*

later. luego. *lweh'-goh*

laundry. lavandería. *lah-ban-deh-ree'-ah*

learn. aprender. *ah-pren-der'*

leather. piel. *pyel'*

leave. salir, irse. *sah-leer', eer'-seh*

left. izquierdo. *eth-kyer'-doh*

leg. pierna. *pyer'-nah*

leisure. tiempo libre. *tyem'-poh lee'-breh*

lemon. limón. *lee-maun'*

less. menos. *meh'-nohs*

letter. carta, letra. *car'-tah, leh'-trah*

lettuce. lechuga. *leh-choo'-gah*

library. biblioteca. *be-blyo-teh'-cah*

life. vida. *bee'-dah*

lift. ascensor. *as-then-saur'*

light. luz, ligero. *looth, le-heh'-roh*

lighter. encendedor. *en-then-deh-daur'*

like. gustar, como. *goos-tar', cau'-moh*

line. línea. *lee'-neh-ah*

lip. labio. *lah'-byo*

listen. escuchar. *es-coo-char'*

little. pequeño, poco. *peh-keh'-nyoh, pau'-coh*

live. vivir. *be-beer'*

liver. hígado. *ee'-gah-doh*

lodging. alojamiento. *ah-lau-hah-myen'-toh*

long. largo. *lar'-goh*

look. mirar. *me-rar'*

look for. buscar. *boos-car'*

lorry. camión. *cah-myon'*

low. bajo. *bah'-hoh*

luggage. equipaje. *eh-ke-pah'-heh*

lunch. almuerzo. *al-mwer'-thoh*

lung. pulmón. *pool-maun'*

machine. máquina.
  mah'-ke-nah
madam. señora. *seh-nyau'-rah*
made. hecho. *eh'-choh*
magazine. revista.
  reh-bees'-tah
mail. correo. *caur-reh'-oh*
main. principal. *prin-the-pahl'*
make. hacer. *ah-thehr'*
man. hombre. *aum'-breh*
many. muchos. *moo'-chohs*
map. mapa. *mah'-pah*
March. marzo. *mar'-thoh*
market. mercado.
  mer-cah'-doh
married. casado/a.
  cah-sah'-doh/-ah
match. cerilla. *theh-ree'-lyah*
mattress. colchón. *caul-chaun'*
May. mayo. *mah'-yoh*
me. mí. *mee*
meal. comida. *cau-mee'-dah*
meat. carne. *car'-neh*
mechanic. mecánico.
  meh-cah'-ne-coh
medicine. medicina.
  meh-de-thee'-nah
melon. melón. *meh-laun'*
mile. milla. *mee'-lyah* (1,6 km)
milk. leche. *leh'-cheh*
million. millón. *me-lyaun'*
minute. minuto. *me-noo'-toh*
mirror. espejo. *es-peh'-hoh*

miss. señorita.
  seh-nyau-ree'-tah
mister. señor. *seh-nhyaur'*
missis. señora. *seh-nyau'-rah*
mixed. mixto/a. *mix'-toh/-ah*
mobile (phone). (teléfono)
  móvil. *(teh-leh'-fau-noh)*
  mau'-beel
moment. momento.
  mau-men'-toh
Monday. lunes. *loo'-nehs*
money. dinero. *de-neh'-roh*
month. mes. *mehs*
monument. monumento.
  mau-noo-men'-toh
more. más. *mas*
morning. mañana.
  mah-nyah'-nah
mother. madre. *mah'-dreh*
motorway. autopista.
  ow-toh-pees'-tah
mountain. montaña.
  maun-tah'-nyah
mouth. boca. *bau'-cah*
much. mucho. *moo'-choh*
museum. museo. *moo-seh'-oh*
music. música. *moo'-se-cah*
my. mi, mis. *mee, mees*

name. nombre. *naum'-breh*
near. cerca. *thehr'-cah*
necessary. necesario.
  neh-theh-sah'-ryo
neck. cuello. *kweh'-lyoh*
need. necesitar.
  neh-theh-se-tar'

neither. ni. *nee*

nephew. sobrino.
sau-bree'-noh

never. nunca. *noon'-cah*

new. nuevo. *nweh'-boh*

news. noticia. *nau-tee'-thya*

newsagent's. quiosco.
kyos'-coh

newspaper. periódico.
peh-ryo'-de-coh

next. próximo, siguiente.
prauc'-se-moh,
se-ghyen'-teh

nice. agradable.
ah-grah-dah'-bleh

niece. sobrina. *sau-bree'-nah*

night. noche. *nau'-cheh*

nine. nueve. *nweh'-beh*

ninety. noventa. *nau-behn'-tah*

no. no, ningún. *noh, nin-goon'*

nobody. nadie. *nah'-dye*

noise. ruido. *rwi'-doh*

none. ninguno/a.
nin-goo'-noh/-ah

noon. mediodía.
meh-dyo-dee'-ah

nor. ni. *nee*

north. norte. *naur'-teh*

nose. nariz. *nah-reeth'*

not. no. *noh*

nothing. nada. *nah'-dah*

November. noviembre.
nau-byem'-breh

now. ahora. *ah-au'-rah*

number. número. *noo'-meh-roh*

nurse. enfermera.
en-fer-meh'-rah

o

o'clock. en punto. *en poon'-toh*

October. octubre. *auc-too'-breh*

of. de. *deh*

office. oficina. *au-fe-thee'-nah*

often. a menudo.
ah meh-noo'-doh

oil. aceite. *ah-theh'-e-teh*

old. viejo. *bye'-hoh*

olive. aceituna.
ah-they-too'-nah

on. en, sobre. *en, sau'-breh*

one. uno. *oo'-noh*

one hundred. cien. *thyen'*

onion. cebolla. *theh-bau'-lyah*

only. sólo, solamente. *sau'-loh,*
sau-lah-men'-teh

open. abierto. *ah-byer'-toh*

opposite. enfrente. *en-fren'-teh*

optician's. óptica. *aup'-te-cah*

or. o. *oh*

orange. naranja. *nah-ran'-hah*

order. orden, pedir. *aur'-den,*
peh-deer'

other. otro/a. *au'-troh/-ah*

ounce. onza. *aun'-thah* (28 g)

our. nuestro. *nwes'-troh*

out. fuera. *fweh'-rah*

out of order. averiado.
ah-beh-rya'-doh

over. encima. *en-thee'-mah*

owner. dueño. *dweh'-nyoh*

package. paquete, bulto.
pah-keh'-teh, bool'-toh

pain. dolor. *dau-laur'*

painting. pintura. *pin-too'-rah*

palace. palacio. *pah-lah'-thyo*

paper. papel. *pah-pehl'*

parcel. paquete. *pah-keh'-teh*

pardon. perdón. *per-daun'*

parents. padres. *pah'-drehs*

park. parque, aparcar.
par'-keh, ah-par-car'

passenger. pasajero.
pah-sah-heh'-roh

passport. pasaporte.
pah-sah-paur'-teh

pavement. acera. *ah-theh'-rah*

pay. pagar. *pah-gar'*

peach. melocotón.
meh-lau-cau-taun'

pear. pera. *peh'-rah*

pedestrian. peatón.
peh-ah-taun'

pen. pluma. *ploo'-mah*

pencil. lápiz. *lah'-peth*

people. gente. *hen'-teh*

pepper. pimienta. *pe-myen'-tah*

permission. permiso.
per-mee'-soh

petrol. gasolina.
gah-sau-lee'-nah

petrol station. gasolinera.
gah-sau-le-neh'-rah

photograph. foto. *fau'-toh*

pick up. recoger. *reh-cau-her'*

picture. cuadro. *kwa'-droh*

pie. pastel, tarta. *pas-tehl',
tar'-tah*

piece. pieza, trozo. *pye'-thah,
trau'-thoh*

pill. pastilla. *pas-tee'-lyah*

pillow. almohada.
al-mau-ah'-dah

pineapple. piña. *pee'-nyah*

pint. pinta. *pin'-tah* (0,5 l)

place. lugar, sitio. *loo-gar',
see'-tyo*

plan. plan. *plahn*

plane. avión. *ah-byon'*

platform. andén. *an-den'*

please. por favor. *paur fah-baur'*

plum. ciruela. *the-rweh'-lah*

pocket. bolsillo. *baul-see'-lyoh*

point. punto. *poon'-toh*

police. policía. *pau-le-thee'-ah*

police station. comisaría.
cau-me-sah-ree'-ah

pork. cerdo. *ther'-doh*

port. puerto. *pwer'-toh*

post office. Correos.
caur-reh'-ohs

potato. patata. *pah-tah'-tah*

pound. libra. *lee'-brah*

prefer. preferir. *preh-feh-reer'*

prescription. receta.
reh-theh'-tah

present. presente, regalo.
preh-sen'-teh, reh-gah'-loh

pretty. guapo, bonito.
gwa'-poh, bau-nee'-toh

price. precio. *preh'-thyo*

problem. problema.
prau-bleh'-mah

promenade. paseo.
pah-seh'-oh

pull. tirar. *te-rar'*

pullover. jersey. *her-seh'-y*

puncture. pinchazo.
pin-chah'-thoh

push. empujar. *em-poo-har'*

put. poner. *pau-ner'*

put in. meter. *meh-ter'*

q

quarter. cuarto. *kwar'-toh*

quay. muelle. *mweh'-lyeh*

question. pregunta.
preh-goon'-tah

queue. cola. *cau'-lah*

quick. rápido. *rah'-pi-doh*

r

rain. llover, lluvia. *lyau-ber',*
lyoo'-bya

reach. llegar. *lyeh-gar'*

read. leer. *leh-er'*

ready. listo. *lees'-toh*

reason. causa, razón.
cah'-oo-sah, rah-thaun'

receive. recibir. *reh-the-beer'*

recommend. recomendar.
reh-cau-men-dar'

red. rojo. *rau'-hoh*

reduction. reducción.
reh-dooc-thyon'

relatives. parientes.
pah-ryen'-tehs

remember. recordar.
reh-caur-dar'

rent. alquilar. *al-ke-lar'*

repair. reparar. *reh-pah-rar'*

repeat. repetir. *reh-peh-teer'*

reply. respuesta. *res-pwes'-tah*

restaurant. restaurante.
res-tow-rahn'-teh

return. volver, vuelta. *baul-ber',*
bwel'-tah

rice. arroz. *ar-rauth'*

right. derecho, correcto.
deh-reh'-choh, caur-rec'-toh

river. río. *ree'-oh*

road. calle, carretera.
cah'-lyeh, car-reh-teh'-rah

roast. asado. *ah-sah'-doh*

room. habitación.
ah-be-tah-thyon'

round. redondo. *reh-daun'-doh*

s

sail. navegar. *nah-beh-gar'*

salad. ensalada. *en-sah-lah'dah*

sale. venta. *ben'-tah*

sales. rebajas. *reh-bah'-hahs*

salt. sal. *sahl*

same. mismo. *mees'-moh*

sand. arena. *ah-reh'-nah*

Saturday. sábado.
sah'-bah-doh

sauce. salsa. *sahl'-sah*

sausage. salchicha.
sahl-chee'-chah

say. decir. *deh-theer'*

school. escuela. *es-kweh'-lah*

sea. mar. *mar*

seafood. marisco. *mah-rees'-coh*

season. estación. *es-tah-thyon'*

seat. asiento. *ah-syen'-toh*

second. segundo. *seh-goon'-doh*

see. ver. *ber*

sell. vender. *ben-der'*

send. mandar, enviar. *man-dar', en-be-ar'*

September. septiembre. *sep-tyem'-breh*

serve. servir. *ser-beer'*

seven. siete. *sye'-the*

seventy. setenta. *seh-tehn'-tah*

several. varios. *bah'-ryos*

she. ella. *eh'-lyah*

sheet. sábana. *sah'-bah-nah*

ship. barco. *bar'-coh*

shirt. camisa. *cah-mee'-sah*

shoe. zapato. *thah-pah'-toh*

shop. tienda. *tyen'-dah*

short. corto. *caur'-toh*

shower. ducha. *doo'-chah*

sick. enfermo/a. *en-fer'-moh/-ah*

side. lado. *lah'-doh*

sign. signo, firmar. *seeg'-noh, fir-mar'*

silence. silencio. *se-len'-thyo*

silver. plata. *plah'-tah*

since. desde. *dehs'-deh*

single. individual, soltero. *in-de-be-dwal', saul-teh'-roh*

sir. señor. *seh-nyaur'*

sister. hermana. *er-mah'-nah*

sit down. sentarse. *sen-tar'-seh*

six. seis. *seys*

sixty. sesenta. *seh-sehn'-tah*

size. talla, tamaño. *tah'-lyah, tah-mah'-nyoh*

sleep. dormir. *daur-meer'*

slow. lento. *len'-toh*

small. pequeño. *peh-keh'-nyoh*

smoke. fumar. *foo-mar'*

snow. nieve. *nye'-beh*

so. así. *ah-see'*

soap. jabón. *hah-baun'*

some. algunos. *ahl-goo'-nohs*

son. hijo. *ee'-hoh*

soon. pronto. *praun'-toh*

sorry. perdón, lo siento. *per-daun', loh syen'-toh*

sort. tipo, clase. *tee'-poh, clah'-seh*

soup. sopa. *sau'-pah*

south. sur. *soor*

souvenir. recuerdo. *reh-kwer'-doh*

Spanish. español. *es-pah-nyaul'*

speak. hablar. *ah-blar'*

speed. velocidad. *beh-lau-the-dad'*

spoon. cuchara. *coo-chah'-rah*

sport. deporte. *deh-paur'-teh*

spring. primavera. *pre-mah-beh'-rah*

square. plaza, cuadrado. *plah'-thah, kwa-drah'-doh*

stairs. escalera.
es-cah-leh'-rah

stamp. sello. *seh'-lyoh*

start. empezar. *em-peh-thar'*

station. estación. *es-tah-thyon'*

steak. filete. *fe-leh'-teh*

stewardess. azafata.
ah-thah-fah'-tah

stomach. estómago.
es-tau'-mah-goh

stop. parar, parada. *pah-rar',*
pah-rah'-dah

strawberry. fresa. *freh'-sah*

street. calle. *cah'-lyeh*

suburb. barrio. *bar'-ryo*

sugar. azúcar. *ah-thoo'-car*

suit. traje. *trah'-heh*

suitcase. maleta. *mah-leh'-tah*

summer. verano. *beh-rah'-noh*

sun. sol. *sohl'*

Sunday. domingo.
dau-meen'-goh

sure. seguro. *seh-goo'-roh*

surgery. consulta.
caun-sool'-tah

surname. apellido.
ah-peh-lyee'-doh

sweet. dulce. *dool'-theh*

swim. nadar. *nah-dar'*

swimming pool. piscina.
pes-thee'-nah

t

table. mesa. *meh'-sah*

tablet. pastilla. *pas-tee'-lyah*

take. tomar, coger. *tau-mar',*
cau-her'

talk. hablar. *ah-blar'*

tall. alto. *ahl'-toh*

tax. impuesto. *im-pwes'-toh*

tea. té. *teh*

telephone. teléfono.
teh-leh'-fau-noh

tell. decir, contar. *deh-theer',*
caun-tar'

temperature. temperatura.
tem-peh-rah-too'-rah

ten. diez. *dyeth'*

tent. tienda de campaña.
tyen'-dah deh
cahm-pah'-nyah

terrace. terraza. *ter-rah'-thah*

than. que. *keh*

thanks. gracias. *grah'-thyas*

that. que. *keh*

the. el, la, los, las. *ehl, lah,*
lohs, lahs

theatre. teatro. *teh-ah'-troh*

their. su, sus. *soo, soos*

there. allí. *ah-lyee'*

these. estos/as. *es'-tohs/-ahs*

think. pensar. *pen-sar'*

thirteen. trece. *treh'-theh*

thirty. treinta. *treh'-in-tah*

this. este/a. *es'-teh/-ah*

thousand. mil. *meel*

three. tres. *tres*

throat. garganta. *gar-gahn'-tah*

Thursday. jueves. *hweh'-behs*

ticket. billete, entrada.
be-lyeh'-teh, en-trah'-dah

tie. corbata. *caur-bah'-tah*

time. tiempo. *tyem'-poh*

tip. propina. *prau-pee'-nah*

to. a, para. *ah, pah'-rah*

toast. tostada. *taus-tah'-dah*

tobacco. tabaco. *tah-bah'-coh*

together. juntos. *hoon'-tohs*

toilets. servicios. *ser-bee'-thyos*

toll. peaje. *peh-ah'-heh*

tomato. tomate. *tau-mah'-teh*

tomorrow. mañana. *mah-nyah'-nah*

tonight. esta noche. *es'-tah nau'-cheh*

too, too much/many. demasiado. *deh-mah-sya'-doh*

tooth. diente. *dyen'-teh*

towel. toalla. *tau-ah'-lyah*

tower. torre. *taur'-reh*

town. ciudad. *thew-dad'*

traffic lights. semáforo. *seh-mah'-fau-roh*

train. tren. *tren*

tram. tranvía. *trahn-bee'-ah*

translate. traducir. *trah-doo-theer'*

travel. viajar, viaje. *bya-har', bya'-heh*

trip. viaje. *bya'-heh*

trousers. pantalones. *pahn-tah-lau'-nehs*

try. tratar, probar. *trah-tar', prau-bar'*

Tuesday. martes. *mar'-tehs*

twelve. doce. *dau'-theh*

twenty. veinte. *beh'-in-teh*

two. dos. *daus*

tyre. neumático. *neh-oo-mah'-te-coh*

u

ugly. feo. *feh'-oh*

umbrella. paraguas. *pah-rah'-gwas*

uncle. tío. *tee'-oh*

under. debajo. *deh-bah'-hoh*

underground. metro. *meh'-troh*

understand. comprender, entender. *caum-pren-der', en-ten-der'*

until. hasta. *as'-tah*

up. arriba. *ar-ree'-bah*

urgent. urgente. *oor-hen'-teh*

use. usar, uso. *oo-sar', oo'-soh*

v

vacant. libre. *lee'-breh*

van. furgoneta. *foor-gau-neh'-tah*

veal. ternera. *ter-neh'-rah*

vegetables. verdura. *ber-doo'-rah*

very. muy. *moo'-y*

view. vista. *bees'-tah*

village. pueblo. *pwe'-bloh*

vinegar. vinagre. *be-nah'-greh*

visa. visado. *be-sah'-doh*

visit. visitar, visita. *be-see-tar', be-see'-tah*

w

wait. esperar. *es-peh-rar'*

walk. andar. *ahn-dar'*

wall. pared. *pah-red'*

wallet. cartera. *car-teh'-rah*

warm. cálido. *cah'-le-doh*

wash. lavar. *lah-bar'*

watch. reloj. *reh-lau'*

water. agua. *ah'-gwa*

way. camino, manera.
   cah-mee'-noh, mah-neh'-rah

we. nosotros. *nau-sau'-trohs*

wear. llevar. *lyeh-bar'*

weather. tiempo. *tyem'-poh*

Wednesday. miércoles.
   myer'-cau-lehs

week. semana. *seh-mah'-nah*

weight. peso. *peh'-soh*

welcome. bienvenido.
   byen-beh-nee'-doh

well. bien. *byen'*

west. oeste. *au-es'-teh*

what. qué, lo que. *keh', loh keh*

wheel. rueda. *rwe'-dah*

when. cuándo. *kwan'-doh*

where. dónde. *daun'-deh*

which. cuál. *kwal'*

white. blanco. *blahn'-coh*

who. quién. *kyen'*

whole. todo. *tau'-doh*

why. por qué. *paur keh'*

wife. esposa, mujer.
   es-pau'-sah, moo-her'

wind. viento. *byen'-toh*

window. ventana. *ben-tah'-nah*

wine. vino. *bee'-noh*

winter. invierno. *in-byer'-noh*

wish. desear. *deh-seh-ar'*

with. con. *caun*

without. sin. *sin*

woman. mujer. *moo-her'*

wool. lana. *lah'-nah*

word. palabra. *pah-lah'-brah*

work. trabajar, trabajo.
   trah-bah-har', trah-bah'-hoh

world. mundo. *moon'-doh*

write. escribir. *es-cre-beer'*

y

yacht. yate. *yah'-teh*

yard. yarda. *yar'-dah* (1,6 km)

year. año. *ah'-nyoh*

yellow. amarillo.
   ah-mah-ree'-lyoh

yes. sí. *see*

yesterday. ayer. *ah-yer'*

you. tú, vosotros. *too,*
   bau-sau'-trohs

young. joven. *jau'-ben*

your. tu, vuestro. *too,*
   bwes'-troh

z

zero. cero. *theh'-roh*

zoo. zoo. *thau'-oh*

a

a. *ah.* to, at

abajo. *ah-bah'-hoh.* down, downstairs

abierto. *ah-byer'-toh.* open

abrigo. *ah-bree'-goh.* coat

abril. *ah-breel'.* April

abrir. *ah-breer'.* open

accidente. *ak-the-den'-teh.* accidente

aceite. *ah-theh'-e-teh.* oil

aceituna. *ah-they-too'-nah.* olive

acelerador.
ah-theh-leh-rah-daur'. accelerator

aceptar. *ah-thep-tar'.* to accept

acera. *ah-theh'-rah.* pavement

aconsejar. *ah-caun-seh-har'.* to advise

acuerdo (de...).
deh ah-kwer'-doh. all right

adiós. *ah-dyos'.* goodbye

aduana. *ah-dwa'-nah.* customs

afeitarse. *ah-fey-tar'-seh.* to shave

agencia. *ah-hen'-thya.* agency

agosto. *ah-gaus'-toh.* August

agradable. *ah-grah-dah'-bleh.* nice

agrio. *ah'-gryo.* sour

agua. *ah'-gwa.* water

ahí. *ah-ee'.* there

ahora. *ah-au'-rah.* now

ahorro. *ah-aur'-roh.* saving

aire. *ah'-e-reh.* air

albaricoque.
al-bah-re-cau'-keh. apricot

alcohol. *al-cau-aul'.* alcohol

algo. *ahl'-goh.* something

algodón. *ahl-gau-daun'.* cotton

almohada. *al-mau-ah'-dah.* pillow

almorzar. *al-maur-thar'.* to have lunch

alojamiento.
ah-lau-hah-myen'-toh. lodging

alquilar. *al-kee-lar'.* to rent, to hire

alto. *ahl'-toh.* tall, high

allí. *ah-lyee'.* there

amable. *ah-mah'-bleh.* kind

amarillo. *ah-mah-ree'-lyoh.* yellow

amargo. *ah-mar'-goh.* bitter

ambulancia.
am-boo-lahn'-thya. ambulance

amigo. *ah-mee'-goh.* friend

andar. *an-dar'.* to walk

andén. *an-den'.* platform

anoche. *ah-nau'-cheh.* last night

antes. *ahn'-tehs.* before

año. *ah'-nyoh.* year

apellido. *ah-peh-lyee'-doh.* surname

aparcar. *ah-par-car'.* to park

aparcamiento.
ah-par-cah-myen'-toh.
parking

apartamento.
ah-par-tah-men'-toh.
apartment

aprender. *ah-pren-der'.*
to learn

aquel. *ah-kehl'.* that

aquí. *ah-kee'.* here

arriba. *ar-ree'-bah.* up, upstairs

arroz. *ar-rauth'.* rice

artesanía. *ar-teh-sah-nee'-ah.*
handicraft

asado. *ah-sah'-doh.* roast

ascensor. *as-then-saur'.* lift

así. *ah-see'.* so

asiento. *ah-syen'-toh.* seat

atención. *ah-ten-thyon'.*
attention

aterrizar. *ah-ter-re-thar'.* to land

atrás. *ah-tras'.* back

atún. *ah-toon'.* tuna

aunque. *ah'-oon-keh.* although

autobús. *ow-tau-boos'.* bus

autocar. *ow-tau-car'.* coach

autopista. *ow-toh-pees'-tah.*
motorway

avería. *ah-beh-ree'-ah.*
breakdown

averiado. *ah-beh-rya'-doh.*
out of order

avión. *ah-byon'.* plane

ayer. *ah-yer'.* yesterday

ayudar. *ah-yoo-dar'.* to help

ayuntamiento.
ah-yoon-tah-myen'-toh.
town hall

azafata. *ah-thah-fah'-tah.*
stewardess

azúcar. *ah-thoo'-car.* sugar

azul. *ah-thool'.* blue

b

bajo. *bah'-hoh.* low, short

banco. *bahn'-coh.* bank

baño. *bah'-nyoh.* bath

barato. *bah-rah'-toh.* cheap

barco. *bar'-coh.* ship

barrio. *bar'-ryo.* district

bastante. *bas-tahn'-teh.* enough

beber. *beh-ber'.* to drink

bebida. *beh-bee'-dah.* drink

biblioteca. *be-blyo-teh'-cah.*
library

bicicleta. *be-the-cleh'-tah.*
bicycle

bien. *byen'.* well

bienvenido.
byen-beh-nee'-doh.
welcome

blanco. *blahn'-coh.* white

boca. *bau'-cah.* mouth

bolso. *baul'-soh.* handbag

bolsillo. *baul-see'-lyoh.* pocket

bonito. *bau-nee'-toh.* pretty

bota. *bau'-tah.* boot

botella. *bau-teh'-lyah.* bottle

brazo. *brah'-thoh.* arm

bueno. *bwe'-noh.* good

buscar. *boos-car'.* to look for

buzón. *boo-thaun'.* letter box

caballero. *cah-bah-lyeh'-roh.* gentleman

cabeza. *cah-beh'-thah.* head

cada. *cah'-dah.* each, every

café. *cah-feh'.* coffee

caja. *cah'-hah.* box, cash

caliente. *cah-lyen'-teh.* hot

calmante. *cal-mahn'-teh.* sedative

calor. *cah-laur'.* heat

calle. *cah'-lyeh.* street

cama. *cah'-mah.* bed

cámara. *cah'-mah-rah.* camera

camarero. *cah-mah-reh'-roh.* waiter

cambiar. *cam-be-ar'.* to change

cambio. *cahm'-byo.* change, exchange

camino. *cah-mee'-noh.* way

camión. *cah-myon'.* lorry

camisa. *cah-mee'-sah.* shirt

campo. *cahm'-poh.* country, field

cara. *cah'-rah.* face

carne. *car'-neh.* meat

carnicería. *car-ne-theh-ree'-ah.* butcher's

caro. *cah'-roh.* expensive

carretera. *car-reh-teh'-rah.* road

carta. *car'-tah.* letter

cartera. *car-the'-rah.* wallet

casado. *cah-sah'-doh.* married

casi. *cah'-see.* almost, nearly

castillo. *cas-tee'-lyoh.* castle

catedral. *cah-teh-drahl'.* cathedral

catorce. *cah-taur'-theh.* fourteen

cebolla. *theh-bau'-lyah.* onion

cena. *theh'-nah.* dinner, supper

cenicero. *theh-ne-theh'-roh.* ashtray

centro. *then'-troh.* centre

cepillo. *theh-pee'-lyoh.* brush

cerca. *ther'-cah.* near

cerdo. *ther'-doh.* pork, pig

cerilla. *theh-ree'-lyah.* match

cero. *theh'-roh.* zero

cerrado. *ther-rah'-doh.* closed

cerrar. *ther-rar'.* to close

cerveza. *ther-beh'-thah.* beer

chaqueta. *chah-keh'-tah.* jacket

cheque. *cheh'-keh.* cheque

chico/a. *chee'-coh/ah.* boy, girl

chocolate. *chau-cau-lah'-teh.* chocolate

chuleta. *choo-leh'-tah.* chop

cielo. *thye'-loh.* sky

cien. *thyen'.* one hundred

cigarrillo. *the-gar-ree'-lyoh.* cigarette

cinco. *theen'-coh.* five

cincuenta. *thin-kwen'-tah.* fifty

cine. *thee'-neh.* cinema

ciruela. *the-rwe'-lah.* plum

cita. *thee'-tah.* apointment

ciudad. *thew-dad'.* town, city

clima. *clee'-mah.* climate

coche. *cau'-cheh.* car

coger. *cau-her'.* to catch, to take

colchón. *caul-chaun'.* mattress

comedor. *cau-meh-daur'.* diningroom

comenzar. *cau-men-thar'.* to begin

comer. *cau-mer'.* to eat

comida. *cau-mee'-dah.* meal, food

comisaría. *cau-me-sah-ree'-ah.* police station

como. *cau'-moh.* how, as, like

comprar. *caum-prar'.* to buy

comprender. *caum-pren-der'.* to understand

con. *caun.* with

conducir. *caun-doo-theer'.* to drive

conmigo. *caun-mee'-goh.* with me

conocer. *cau-nau-thehr'.* to know

consigna. *caun-seeg'-nah.* left-luggage office

consulado. *caun-soo-lah'-doh.* consulate

consulta. *caun-sool'-tah.* surgery

contento. *caun-ten'-toh.* glad

contestar. *caun-tes-tar'.* to answer

contigo. *caun-tee'-goh.* with you

contra. *caun'-trah.* against

copa. *cau'-pah.* (wine).glass

corazón. *cau-rah-thaun'.* heart

corbata. *caur-bah'-tah.* tie

correo. *caur-reh'-oh.* mail

Correos. *caur-reh'-ohs.* post office

cortar. *caur-tar'.* to cut

corto. *caur'-toh.* short

cosa. *cau'-sah.* thing

costa. *caus'-tah.* coast

cotización. *cau-te-thah-thyon'.* rate

crema. *creh'-mah.* cream

cristal. *crees-tahl'.* glass, lens

cruce. *croo'-theh.* croosroads

cuadro. *kwa'-droh.* picture

cuál. *kwal'.* which

cualquiera. *kwal-kye'-rah.* any

cuando. *kwan'-doh.* when

cuánto. *kwan'-toh.* how much/many

cuarenta. *kwa-ren'-tah.* forty

cuarto. *coo-ar'-toh.* quarter, fourth, room

cuatro. *kwa'-troh.* four

cubierta. *coo-byer'-tah.* cover, deck

cuchara. *coo-chah'-rah.* spoon

cuchillo. *coo-chee'-lyoh.* knife

cuello. *kwe'-lyoh.* neck, collar

cuenta. *kwen'-tah.* bill, account

cuerpo. *kwer'-poh.* body

cuidado. *kwi-dah'-doh.* care, attention

curva. *coor'-bah.* bend, curve

dar. *dar.* to give

de. *deh.* of, from

debajo. *deh-bah'-hoh.* down, downstairs

decir. *deh-theer'.* to say, to tell

dedo. *deh'-doh.* finger, toe

delante. *deh-lahn'-teh.* in front

demasiado. *deh-mah-sya'-doh.* too, too much/many

dentro. *den'-troh.* inside

deporte. *deh-paur'-teh.* sport

desayuno. *deh-sah-yoo'-noh.* breakfast

descuento. *des-kwen'-toh.* discount

desde. *des'-deh.* from

desear. *deh-seh-ar'.* to want

despacio. *des-pah'-thyo.* slowly

después. *des-pwes'.* after

detrás. *deh-tras'.* behind

día. *dee'-ah.* day

diario. *dya'-ryo.* daily

dibujo. *deh-boo'-hoh.* drawing

diccionario. *dek-thyo-nah'-ryo.* dictionary

diciembre. *de-thyem'-breh.* December

diente. *dyen'-teh.* tooth

diez. *dyeth'.* ten

difícil. *de-fee'-thil.* difficult

dinero. *de-neh'-roh.* money

dirección. *de-rek-thyon'.* direction, address

diversión. *de-ber-syon'.* entertainment

divisa. *de-bee'-sah.* foreign currency

doce. *dau'-theh.* twelve

docena. *dau-theh'-nah.* dozen

dólar. *dau'-lar.* dollar

dolor. *dau-laur'.* pain, ache

domingo. *dau-meen'-goh.* Sunday

donde. *daun'-deh.* where

dormir. *daur-meer'.* to sleep

dormitorio. *daur-me-tau'-ryo.* bedroom

dos. *daus.* two

ducha. *doo'-chah.* shower

dulce. *dool'-theh.* sweet

durar. *doo-rar'.* to last

edad. *eh-dad'.* age

edificio. *eh-de-fee'-thyo.* building

ejemplo. *eh-hehm'-ploh.* example

el. *ehl.* the

él. *el.* he

ella. *eh'-lyah.* she

embajada. *em-bah-hah'-dah.* embassy

empezar. *em-peh-thar'.* to begin, to start

empujar. *em-poo-har'.* to push

en. *ehn.* in, on

encendedor. *en-then-deh-daur'.* lighter

encima. *en-thee'-mah.* above, over

encontrar. *en-caun-trar'.* to find, to meet

enero. *eh-neh'-roh.* January

enfermedad. *en-fer-meh-dad'.* illness, disease

enfermera. *en-fer-meh'-rah.* nurse

enfermo. *en-fer'-moh.* ill, sick

enfrente. *en-fren'-teh.* opposite

ensalada. *en-sah-lah'-dah.* salad

enseñar. *en-seh-nyar'.* to teach, to show

entender. *en-ten-der'.* to understand

entero. *en-teh'-roh.* whole

entrada. *en-trah'-dah.* entrance, ticket

entre. *en'-treh.* between, among

enviar. *en-be-ar'.* to send

equipaje. *eh-ke-pah'-heh.* luggage

error. *er-raur'.* mistake

escalera. *es-cah-leh'-rah.* stairs

escribir. *es-cre-beer'.* to write

escuchar. *es-coo-char'.* to listen

escuela. *es-kwe'-lah.* school

ese. *eh'-seh.* that

espalda. *es-pahl'-dah.* back

español. *es-pah-nyaul'.* Spanish

espectáculo. *es-pek-tah'-coo-loh.* show

espejo. *es-peh'-hoh.* mirror

esperar. *es-peh-rar'.* to wait, to hope

esquina. *es-kee'-nah.* corner

estación. *es-tah-thyon'.* station, season

estanco. *es-tahn'-coh.* tobacconist's

estar. *es-tar'.* to be

este. *es'-teh.* this, East

estómago. *es-tau'-mah-goh.* stomach

estreñimiento. *es-treh-nye-myen'-toh.* constipation

euro. *eh'-oo-roh.* euro

exposición. *ex-pau-se-thyon'.* exhibition

extranjero. *ex-tran-heh'-roh.* foreign(er)

f

fácil. *fah'-thil.* easy

factura. *fac-too'-rah.* invoice

falda. *fahl'-dah.* skirt

familia. *fah-mee'-lya.* family

farmacia. *far-mah'-thya.* chemist's

favor (por...). *paur fah-baur'.* please

febrero. *feh-breh'-roh.* February

fecha. *feh'-chah.* date

feliz. *feh-leeth'.* happy

feo. *feh'-oh.* ugly

fiebre. *fye'-breh.* fever

fiesta. *fyes'-tah.* party

fila. *fee'-lah.* row, line

filete. *fe-leh'-teh.* steak

fin(al). *feen, fe-nahl'.* end

firmar. *fer-mar'.* to sign

flor. *flaur.* flower

folleto. *fau-lyeh'-toh.* brochure

foto. *fau'-toh.* photograph

fresa. *freh'-sah.* strawberry

fresco. *fres'-coh.* cool, fresh

frío. *free'-oh.* cold

frito. *free'-toh.* fried

frontera. *fraun-teh'-rah.* frontier

fruta. *froo'-tah.* fruit

fuego. *fwe'-goh.* fire

fuente. *fwen'-teh.* fountain

fuera. *fwe'-rah.* out, outside

fumar. *foo-mar'.* to smoke

furgoneta. *foor-gau-neh'-tah.*
   van

g

gafas. *gah'-fahs.* glasses

galleta. *gah-lyeh'-tah.* biscuit

garganta. *gar-gahn'-tah.* throat

gasolina. *gah-sau-lee'-nah.*
   petrol

gasolinera.
   gah-sau-le-neh'-rah.
   petrol station

gazpacho. *gath-pah'-choh.*
   vegetable cold soup

gente. *hen'-teh.* people

gracias. *grah'-thyas.* thanks

grado. *grah'-doh.* degree

gran(de). *grahn'(deh).* big,
   great, large

gratis. *grah'-tees.* free

gripe. *gree'-peh.* influenza

gris. *grees.* grey

guía. *ghee'-ah.* guide

gustar. *goos-tar'.* to like

h

haber. *ah-ber'.* *to have*

habitación. *ah-be-tah-thyon'.*
   room

hablar. *ah-blar'.* to speak,
   to talk

hacer. *ah-thehr'.* to do, to make

hambre. *ahm'-breh.* hunger

hasta. *as'-tah.* until

hecho. *eh'-choh.* fact, done,
   made

helado. *eh-lah'-doh.* ice-cream

herido. *eh-ree'-doh.* injured,
   wounded

hermano/a. *er-mah'-noh/ah.*
   brother, sister

hielo. *ye'-loh.* ice

hígado. *ee'-gah-doh.* liver

hijo/a. *ee'-hoh/-ah.* son,
   daughter

hola. *au'-lah.* hello

hombre. *aum'-breh.* man

hora. *au'-rah.* hora

hospital. *aus-pe-tahl'.* hospital

hotel. *au-tehl'.* hotel

hoy. *au'-y.* today

huelga. *wel'-gah.* strike

hueso. *we'-soh.* bone
huevo. *we'-boh.* egg

i

idioma. *e-dyo'-mah.* language
iglesia. *e-gleh'-sya.* church
igual. *e-gwal'.* same, equal
impuesto. *im-pwes'-toh.* tax
incluido. *in-klwi'-doh.* included
individual. *in-de-be-dwal'.*
  single
información.
  in-faur-mah-thyon'.
  information
inglés. *in-glés.* English
invitar. *in-be-tar'.* to try
interés. *in-teh-res'.* interest
interesante.
  in-teh-reh-sahn'-teh.
  interesting
intérprete. *in-ter'-preh-teh.*
  interpreter
invierno. *in-byer'-noh.* winter
ir. *eer.* to go
isla. *ees'-lah.* island
izquierdo. *ith-kyer'-doh.* left

j

jabón. *hah-baun'.* soap
jamón. *hah-maun'.* ham
jarabe. *hah-rah'-beh.* syrup
jardín. *har-deen'.* garden
jersey. *her-seh'-y.* pullover
joven. *hau'-ben.* young
joya. *hau'-yah.* jewel
joyería. *hau-yeh-ree'-ah.*
  jeweller's
jueves. *hwe'-behs.* Thursday

juguete. *hoo-gheh'-teh.* toy
julio. *hoo'-lyo.* July
junio. *hoo'-nyo.* June
juntos. *hoon'-tohs.* together

k

kilo(gramo).
  kee'-loh(grah-moh). kilo
kilómetro. *kee-lau'-meh-troh.*
  kilometre

l

la. *lah.* the (fem.), her
labio. *lah'-byo.* lip
lado. *lah'-doh.* side
lámpara. *lahm'-pah-rah.* lamp
lana. *lah'-nah.* wool
lápiz. *lah'-pith.* pencil
largo. *lar'-goh.* long
lata. *lah'-tah.* tin, can
lavar. *lah-bar'.* to wash
lavandería.
  lah-ban-deh-ree'-ah. laundry
le. *leh.* him, her
leche. *leh'-cheh.* milk
lechuga. *leh-choo'-gah.* lettuce
leer. *leh-er'.* to read
lejos. *leh'-hohs.* far
lengua. *len'-gwa.* language,
  tongue
lento. *len'-toh.* slow
libre. *lee'-breh.* free, vacant
librería. *le-breh-ree'-ah.*
  bookshop
libra. *lee'-brah.* pound
libro. *lee'-broh.* book
llmón. *le-maun'.* lemon
limpio. *leem'-pyo.* clean

línea. *lee'-neh-ah.* line

litera. *le-teh'-rah.* couchette

llamada. *lyah-mah'-dah.* call

llamar. *lyah-mar'.* to call, to phone

llave. *lyah'-beh.* key

lleno. *lyeh'-noh.* full

llegada. *lyeh-gah'-dah.* arrival

llegar. *lyeh-gar'.* to arrive

llevar. *lyeh-bar'.* to carry, to wear

llover. *lyau-ber'.* to rain

lluvia. *lyoo'-bya.* rain

lo. *loh.* it, him

lomo. *lau'-moh.* loin

luego. *lwe'-goh.* later

lugar. *loo-gar'.* place

lunes. *loo'-nehs.* Monday

luz. *looth.* light

m

madre. *mah'-dreh.* mother

mal. *mahl.* bad, badly

maleta. *mah-leh'-tah.* suitcase

malo. *mah'-loh.* bad

mandar. *man-dar'.* to send

manera. *mah-neh'-rah.* way, manner

mano. *mah'-noh.* hand

manta. *mahn'-tah.* blanket

mantequilla. *man-teh-kee'-lyah.* butter

manzana. *man-thah'-nah.* apple

mañana. *mah-nyah'-nah.* tomorrow, morning

mapa. *mah'-pah.* map

máquina. *mah'-ke-nah.* machine

mar. *mar.* sea

mareo. *mah-reh'-oh.* seasickness

marido. *mah-ree'-doh.* husband

marisco. *mah-rees'-coh.* seafood

marrón. *mar-raun'.* brown

martes. *mar'-tehs.* Tuesday

marzo. *mar'-thoh.* March

más. *mas.* more

matrícula. *mah-tree'-coo-lah.* number-plate

mayo. *mah'-yoh.* May

me. *meh.* me

mecánico. *meh-cah'-ne-coh.* mechanic

medianoche. *meh-dya-nau'-cheh.* midnight

medicina. *meh-de-thee'-nah.* medicine

médico. *meh'-de-coh.* doctor

medida. *meh-dee'-dah.* measure

medio. *meh'-dyo.* half, middle

mediodía. *meh-dyo-dee'-ah.* midday, noon

mejor. *meh-haur'.* better, best

melocotón. *meh-lau-cau-taun'.* peach

melón. *meh-laun'.* melon

menos. *meh'-nohs.* less, least

menudo (a...).
ah meh-noo'-doh. often

mercado. *mer-cah'-doh.* market

mermelada. *mer-meh-lah'-dah.* jam

mes. *mes.* month

mesa. *meh'-sah.* table

metro. *meh'-troh.* metre, underground

mezcla. *meth'-clah.* mixture

mi. *mee.* my

mí. *mee'.* me

miel. *myel'.* honey

miércoles. *myer'-cau-lehs.* Wednesday

mil. *meel.* thousand

milla. *mee'-lyah.* mile

millón. *me-lyaun'.* million

minuto. *me-noo'-toh.* minute

mío/a. *mee'-oh/-ah.* mine

mirar. *me-rar'.* to look

mismo. *mees'-moh.* same

mitad. *me-tad'.* half

mixto. *meex'-toh.* mixed

momento. *mau-men'-toh.* moment

moneda. *mau-neh'-dah.* coin, currency

montaña. *maun-tah'-nyah.* mountain

monumento.
mau-noo-men'-toh. monument

motivo. *mau-tee'-boh.* reason

moto. *mau'-toh.* Motorcycle

móvil. *mau'-beel.* mobile (phone)

muchacho/a.
moo-chah'-choh/ah. boy, girl

mucho. *moo'-choh.* much

muelle. *mwe'-lyeh.* quay

mujer. *moo-her'.* woman, wife

multa. *mool'-tah.* fine

museo. *moo-seh'-oh.* museum

música. *moo'-se-cah.* music

muy. *moo'-y.* very

n

nacimiento.
nah-the-myen'-toh. birth

nada. *nah'-dah.* nothing

nadar. *nah-dar'.* to swim

nadie. *nah'-dye.* nobody

naranja. *nah-rahn'-hah.* orange

nariz. *nah-rith'.* nose

nata. *nah'-tah.* cream

Navidad. *nah-be-dad'.* Christmas

necesario. *neh-theh-sah'-ryo.* necessary

necesitar. *neh-theh-se-tar'.* to need

negro. *neh'-groh.* black

neumático.
neh-oo-mah'-te-coh. tyre

nevar. *neh-bar'.* to snow

ni. *nee.* nor, neither

niebla. *nye'-blah.* fog

nieve. *nye'-beh.* snow

ningún/a. *nen-goon'/ah.* no, not any

niño/a. *nee'-noh/ah.* child

no. *noh.* no, not

noche. *nau'-cheh.* night

nombre. *naum'-breh.* name, noun

norte. *naur'-teh.* north

nos. *nohs.* us

nosotros. *nau-sau'-trohs.* we

noticia. *nau-tee'-thya.* news

noventa. *nau-behn'-tah.* ninety

noviembre. *nau-byem'-breh.* November

novio/a. *noh'-byoh/-ah.* boyfriend/girlfriend

nube. *noo'-beh.* cloud

nuestro. *nwes'-troh.* our, ours

nueve. *nwe'-beh.* nine

nuevo. *nwe'-boh.* new

número. *noo'-meh-roh.* number

nunca. *noon'-cah.* never

o

o. *oh.* or

obra. *au'-brah.* work, play

ochenta. *au-chehn'-tah.* eighty

ocho. *au'-choh.* eight

ocio. *au'-thyo.* leisure

octubre. *auc-too'-breh.* October

ocupado. *au-coo-pah'-doh.* occupied

oeste. *au-es'-teh.* west

oferta. *au-fer'-tah.* offer

oficina. *au-fe-thee'-nah.* office

ofrecer. *au-freh-thehr'.* to offer

oído. *oy'-doh.* ear

oír. *oyr'.* to hear

ojo. *au'-hoh.* eye

olvidar. *aul-be-dar'.* to forget

once. *aun'-theh.* eleven

óptica. *aup'-te-cah.* optician's

orden. *aur'-den.* order

oreja. *au-reh'-hah.* ear

oro. *au'-roh.* gold

os. *aus.* you

otoño. *au-tau'-nyoh.* autumn

otro. *au'-troh.* another, other

p

padre. *pah'-dreh.* father

padres. *pah'-drehs.* parents

pagar. *pah-gar'.* to pay

país. *pah-ees'.* country

paisaje. *pah-e-sah'-heh.* landscape

palabra. *pah-lah'-brah.* word

palacio. *pah-lah'-thyo.* palace

pan. *pahn.* bread

panadería. *pah-nah-deh-ree'-ah.* baker's

pantalones. *pan-tah-lau'-nehs.* trousers

papel. *pah-pehl'.* paper

paquete. *pah-keh'-teh.* parcel, package

para. *pah'-rah.* to, in order to, for

parada. *pah-rah'-dah.* stop

paraguas. *pah-rah'-gwas.* umbrella

parar. *pah-rar'.* to stop

pared. *pah-red'.* wall

pariente. *pah-ryen'-teh.* relative

parque. *par'-keh.* park

pasajero. *pah-sah-heh'-roh.* passenger

pasaporte. *pah-sah-paur'-teh.* passport

paseo. *pah-seh'-oh.* walk, promenade

pastel. *pas-tehl'.* pie, cake

pastilla. *pas-tee'-lyah.* tablet

patata. *pah-tah'-tah.* potato

peaje. *peh-ah'-heh.* toll

peatón. *peh-ah-taun'.* pedestrian

pecho. *peh'-choh.* chest

pedazo. *peh-dah'-thoh.* piece, bit

pedir. *peh-deer'.* to ask for, to order

peine. *peh'-e-neh.* comb

película. *peh-lee'-coo-lah.* film

peligro. *peh-lee'-groh.* danger

peligroso. *peh-le-grau'-soh.* dangerous

pelo. *peh'-loh.* hair

peluquería. *peh-loo-keh-ree'-ah.* hairdresser's

pensar. *pen-sar'.* to think

pensión. *pen-syon'.* boarding-house

pequeño. *peh-keh'-nyoh.* little, small

pera. *peh'-rah.* pear

perder. *per-der'.* to lose

perdón. *per-daun'.* pardon, sorry

periódico. *peh-ryo'-de-coh.* newspaper

permiso. *per-mee'-soh.* permission, licence

pero. *peh'-roh.* but

pescado. *pes-cah'-doh.* fish

peso. *peh'-soh.* weight

pie. *pye'.* foot

piedra. *pye'-drah.* stone

piel. *pyel'.* skin, leather

pierna. *pyer'-nah.* leg

pila. *pee'-lah.* battery

pimienta. *pe-myen'-tah.* pepper

pimiento. *pe-myen'-toh.* (red, green) pepper

pinchazo. *pin-chah'-thoh.* puncture

pintura. *pin-too'-rah.* painting

piña. *pee'-nyah.* pineapple

piscina. *pes-thee'-nah.* swimming pool

piso. *pee'-soh.* flat, floor

planchar. *plan-char'.* to iron

plano. *plah'-noh.* street map

planta. *plahn'-tah.* plant, floor

plata. *plah'-tah.* silver

plátano. *plah'-tah-noh.* banana

plato. *plah'-toh.* dish

playa. *plah'-yah.* beach

plaza. *plah'-thah.* square

pluma. *ploo'-mah.* pen

poco. *pau'-coh.* little, few

poder. *pau-der'.* can, may

policía. *pau-le-thee'-ah.* police, policeman

pollo. *pau'-lyoh.* chicken

poner. *pau-ner'.* to put

poquito. *pau-kee'-toh.* little

por. *paur.* by, for, because of

porque. *paur'-keh.* because

por qué. *paur keh'.* why

postal. *paus-tahl'.* postcard

postre. *paus'-treh.* dessert

precio. *preh'-thyo.* price

pregunta. *preh-goon'-tah.* question

preguntar. *preh-goon-tar'.* to ask

prensa. *pren'-sah.* press

preparar. *preh-pah-rar'.* to prepare

presentar. *preh-sen-tar'.* to introduce

primavera. *pre-mah-beh'-rah.* spring

primero. *pre-meh'-roh.* first

primo. *pree'-moh.* cousin

principal. *prin-the-pahl'.* main

prisa. *pree'-sah.* hurry

problema. *pro-bleh'-mah.* problem

prohibir. *prau-e-beer'.* to forbid

pronto. *praun'-toh.* soon

propina. *prau-pee'-nah.* tip

próximo. *prauc'-se-moh.* next, close

pueblo. *pwe'-bloh.* village

puente. *pwen'-teh.* bridge

puerta. *pwer'-tah.* door

puerto. *pwer'-toh.* port, harbour

pulmón. *pool-maun'.* lung

q

que. *keh.* that, what

qué. *keh'.* what, which

quedarse. *keh-dar'-seh.* to stay

queja. *keh'-hah.* complaint

quemadura. *keh-mah-doo'-rah.* burn

querer. *keh-rer'.* to want, to love

queso. *keh'-soh.* cheese

quien. *kyen'.* who

quince. *keen'-theh.* fifteen

quinientos. *ke-nyen'-tohs.* five hundred

quinto. *keen'-toh.* fifth

quiosco. *kyos'-coh.* newsagent's

r

rápido. *rah'-pe-doh.* quick

rebajas. *reh-bah'-hahs.* sales

receta. *reh-theh'-tah.* prescription, recipe

recibir. *reh-the-beer'.* to receive

reclamar. *reh-clah-mar'.* to claim

recoger. *reh-cau-her'.* to collect, to pick up

188

recomendar. *reh-cau-men-dar'.* to recommend, to advise

recordar. *reh-caur-dar'.* to remember

recto. *rek'-toh.* straight

recuerdo. *reh-kwer'-doh.* souvenir, regard

redondo. *reh-daun'-doh.* round

refresco. *reh-fres'-coh.* refreshment

regalo. *reh-gah'-loh.* present, gift

reloj. *reh-lau'.* watch

reparar. *reh-pah-rar'.* to repair

repetir. *reh-peh-teer'.* to repeat

repuesto. *reh-pwes'-toh.* spare

reservar. *reh-ser-bar'.* to book, to reserve

resfriado. *res-frya'-doh.* cold

respuesta. *res-pwes'-tah.* answer

restaurante. *res-tow-rahn'-teh.* restaurant

retraso. *reh-trah'-soh.* delay

revista. *reh-bees'-tah.* magazine

riñón. *rə-nyaun'.* kidney

río. *ree'-oh.* river

rodilla. *rau-dee'-lyah.* knee

rojo. *rau'-hoh.* red

ropa. *rau'-pah.* clothes

rosa. *rau'-sah.* rose, pink

roto. *rau'-toh.* broken

rubio. *roo'-byo.* blond

rueda. *rwe'-dah.* wheel

ruido. *rwi'-doh.* noise

s

sábado. *sah'-bah-doh.* Saturday

sábana. *sah'-bah-nah.* sheet

saber. *sah-ber'.* to know

sal. *sahl.* salt

sala. *sah'-lah.* hall

salida. *sah-lee'-dah.* departure, exit

salir. *sah-leer'.* to go out, to leave

salón. *sah-laun'.* living room

salsa. *sahl'-sah.* sauce

salud. *sah-lood'.* health, cheers

sangre. *sahn'-greh.* blood

se. *seh.* oneself, him/herself

seco. *seh'-coh.* dry

sed. *sehd'.* thirst

seguir. *seh-gheer'.* to follow, to go on

segundo. *seh-goon'-doh.* second

seguro. *seh-goo'-roh.* sure, safe

seis. *seh'-ees.* six

sello. *seh'-lyoh.* stamp

semana. *seh-mah'-nah.* week

semáforo. *seh-mah'-fau-roh.* traffic-lights

sentarse. *sen-tar'-seh.* to sit down

señal. *seh-nyahl'.* signal, sign

señor. *seh-nyaur'.* mister, sir

señora. *seh-nyau'-rah.* Mrs., madam

septiembre. *sep-tyem'-breh.* September

ser. *ser.* to be

servicio. *ser-bee'-thyo.* service

servicios. *ser-bee'-thyos.* toilets

servilleta. *ser-be-lyeh'-tah.* serviette

servir. *ser-beer'.* to serve

sesenta. *seh-sehn'-tah.* sixty

setenta. *seh-tehn'-tah.* seventy

si. *see.* if, whether

sí. *see'.* yes

siempre. *syem'-preh.* always

siete. *sye'-teh.* seven

siglo. *see'-gloh.* century

siguiente. *se-ghyen'-teh.* next, following

silencio. *se-len'-thyo.* silence

silla. *see'-lyah.* chair

simpático. *sem-pah'-te-coh.* nice

sin. *sin.* without

sitio. *see'-tyo.* place, spot

sobre. *sau'-breh.* over, envelope

sobrino/a. *sau-bree'-noh/ah.* nephew, niece

socorro. *sau-caur'-roh.* help, aid

sol. *saul.* sun

solamente. *sau-lah-men'-teh.* only

solo. *sau'-loh.* alone, only

soltero. *saul-teh'-roh.* single, unmarried

sopa. *sau'-pah.* soup

su. *soo.* his, her, its, their

subir. *soo-beer'.* to go up

sucio. *soo'-thyo.* dirty

suelo. *swe'-loh.* floor, ground

suerte. *swer'-teh.* luck

sur. *soor.* south

suyo. *soo'-yoh.* his, hers, theirs

t

tabaco. *tah-bah'-coh.* tobacco

talla. *tah'-lyah.* size

taller. *tah-lyer'.* repair shop

tamaño. *tah-mah'-nyoh.* size

también. *tam-byen'.* also, too

tampoco. *tam-pau'-coh.* not either

tan. *tahn.* so, as

tanto. *tahn'-toh.* so much/many

tapa. *tah-pah.* small dish of food

taquilla. *tah-kee'-lyah.* ticket office

tarde. *tar'-deh.* afternoon, late

tarifa. *tah-ree'-fah.* rate

tarjeta. *tar-heh'-tah.* card

tarta. *tar'-tah.* cake, tart

taza. *tah'-thah.* cup

te. *teh.* you, yourself

té. *teh'.* tea

teatro. *teh-ah'-troh.* theatre

teléfono. *teh-leh'-fau-noh.* telephone

televisión. *teh-leh-be-syon'.* TV

temperatura. *tem-peh-rah-too'-rah.* temperature

temprano. *tem-prah'-noh.* early

tenedor. *teh-neh-daur'.* fork

tener. *teh-nehr'.* to have, to possess

tercero. *ter-theh'-roh.* third

terminar. *ter-me-nar'.* to finish

ternera. *ter-neh'-rah.* veal

terraza. *ter-rah'-thah.* terrace

ti. *tee.* you

tiempo. *tyem-poh.* time, weather

tienda. *tyen'-dah.* shop, tent

tinto. *teen'-toh.* red (wine)

tío/a. *tee'-oh/ah.* uncle, aunt

típico. *tee'-pe-coh.* typical

tirar. *tee-rar'.* to pull, to throw

toalla. *tau-ah'-lyah.* towel

todavía. *tau-dah-bee'-ah.* still, yet

todo. *tau'-doh.* all, the whole

tomar. *tau-mar'.* to take

tomate. *tau-mah'-teh.* tomato

torero. *tau-reh'-roh.* bullfighter

toro. *tau'-roh.* bull

torre. *taur'-reh.* tower

tortilla. *taur-tee'-lyah.* omelet

tos. *taus.* cough

tostada. *taus-tah'-dah.* toast

trabajar. *trah-bah-har'.* to work

traducir. *trah-doo-theer'.* to translate

traer. *trah-er'.* to bring

traje. *trah'-heh.* dress, suit

tranquilo. *tran-kee'-loh.* quiet

tranvía. *tran-bee'-ah.* tram

travesía. *trah-beh-see'-ah.* crossing

trece. *treh'-theh.* thirteen

treinta. *treh'-in-tah.* thirty

tren. *trehn.* train

tres. *trehs.* three

trozo. *trau'-thoh.* piece, part

tu. *too.* your

tú. *too'.* you

turismo. *too-rees'-moh.* tourism

turista. *too-rees'-tah.* tourist

tuyo. *too'-yoh.* yours

u

último. *ool'-te-moh.* last, final

un/a. *oon/ah.* a, an

único. *oo'-ne-coh.* only (one)

uno. *oo'-noh.* one

urgente. *oor-hen'-teh.* urgent

usted. *oos-ted'.* you

uva. *oo'-bah.* grape

v

vacaciones. *bah-cah-thyo'-nehs.* holidays

vacío. *bah-thee'-oh.* empty

vagón. *bah-gaun'.* coach

vale. *bah'-leh.* OK

valer. *bah-ler'.* to cost

vaqueros. *bah-keh'-rohs.* jeans

varios. *bah'-ryos.* several

vaso. *bah'-soh.* glass

veinte. *beh'-in-teh.* twenty

velocidad. *beh-lau-the-dad'.* speed

vender. *ben-der'.* to sell

venir. *beh-neer'.* to come

venta. *ben'-tah.* sale

ventana. *ben-tah'-nah.* window

ventanilla. *ben-tah-nee'-lyah.* ticket/car window

ver. *ber.* to see

verano. *beh-rah'-noh.* summer

verde. *ber'-deh.* green

verdura. *ber-doo'-rah.* vegetables

vestido. *bes-tee'-doh.* dress

vía. *bee'-ah.* track

viajar. *bya-har'.* to travel

viaje. *bya'-heh.* travel, trip

viajero. *bya-heh'-roh.* traveller

viejo. *bye'-hoh.* old

viento. *byen'-toh.* wind

viernes. *byer'-nehs.* Friday

vinagre. *be-nah'-greh.* vinegar

vino. *bee'-noh.* wine

visado. *be-sah'-doh.* visa

visita. *be-see'-tah.* visit

visitar. *be-see-tar'.* to visit

vista. *bees'-tah.* view, sight

viudo/a. *bew'-doh/ah.* widow(er)

vivir. *be-beer'.* to live

volver. *baul-ber'.* to return

vosotros. *bau-sau'-trohs.* you

vuelo. *bwe'-loh.* flight

vuelta. *bwel'-tah.* return, turn

vuestro. *bwes'-troh.* your, yours

y

y. *ee.* and

ya. *yah.* already

yate. *yah'-teh.* yacht

yo. *yoh.* I

z

zanahoria. *thah-nah-au'-rya.* carrot

zapatería. *thah-pah-teh-ree'-ah.* shoe shop

zapato. *thah-pah'-toh.* shoe

zoo. *thau'-oh.* zoo

zumo. *thoo'-moh.* juice